75 TH ANNUAL Writer's Digest Writing Competition

COLLECTION

The Grand-Prize and First-Place Manuscripts in each category of the 75th Annual *Writer's Digest* Writing Competition

90067 • *Writer's Digest* • 4700 East Galbraith Road • Cincinnati, OH 45236

Outskirts Press
http://www.outskirtspress.com

ISBN-10: 1-4327-0010-3
ISBN-13: 978-1-4327-0010-2

INTꞄODUCTION

The editors of *Writer's Digest* are pleased to share with you the winning entries in each category of the 75th Annual *Writer's Digest* Writing Competition, along with the Grand Prize-winning story, "House on Fire," by Mary Feuer.

A special thanks goes to our esteemed panel of final-round judges:

- **Nancy Bilyeau** (Feature Article) is an articles editor at *Ladies' Home Journal*. She's also been an editor on the staff of *Good Housekeeping, Rolling Stone, Men's Journal, Healthy Living, Mademoiselle* and *American Film*. She wrote a chapter for Therese J. Borchard's *The Imperfect Mom: Candid Confessions of Mothers Living in the Real World*, which was published by Broadway in April 2006.

- **Aron Eli Coleite** (Stage Play) writes for the NBC forensic drama *Crossing Jordan*. He recently crossed the border of reality in writing/producing *Urban Arcana*, a TV series for the Sci-Fi Channel based on the Hasbro role-playing game. His play *The Family Room* recently garnered Critic's Choice from *Backstage West* and *LA Weekly*.

- **Jennifer Crusie** (Genre Short Story) is the author of 16 novels, one book of literary criticism, miscellaneous articles, essays, novellas, and short stories, and the editor of two nonfiction anthologies. She's been on the bestselling lists of *The New York Times, USA Today* and *Publishers Weekly*. She lives in Ohio, where she often stares at the ceiling and counts her blessings.

- **Hollis Gillespie** (Memoir/Personal Essay) is the award-winning syndicated humor columnist and NPR commentator who penned the popular book *Bleachy-Haired Honky Bitch: Tales from a Bad Neighborhood* (Regan Books) and its sequel, *Confessions of a Recovering Slut and Other Love Stories* (Regan Books). A *Writer's Digest* 2004 Breakout Author of the Year, Gillespie lives in Atlanta, only now on a street out of stray-bullet range from her old neighborhood.

- **Jerry B. Jenkins** (Inspirational) is a novelist (the *Left Behind* series), biographer (Hank Aaron, Walter Payton, Billy Graham), and marriage and family author (*Hedges: Loving Your Marriage Enough to Protect It* [Crossway]). He's written more than 150 books and owns Jenkins Entertainment—a filmmaking company in Los Angeles—and the Christian Writers Guild.

- **Dorianne Laux** (Non-rhyming Poetry) is the author of four books of poetry, most recently *Facts About the Moon* (W.W. Norton). She's also co-author of *The Poet's Companion: A Guide to the Pleasures of Writing Poetry* (W.W. Norton). She's a professor at the University of Oregon and also teaches at

Pacific University's Low Residency Program in Forest Grove, Ore.

- **Warren Littlefield** (Television/Movie Script) spent 10 years as president of NBC Entertainment, where he was responsible for the development of such shows as *Seinfeld, Friends, Will & Grace* and *ER*. He currently heads the Littlefield Company, where he's produced *Do Over* (WB), *Keen Eddie* (FOX), *Like Family* (WB) and *Love, Inc.* (UPN).

- **Carol Moldaw** (Rhyming Poetry) is the author of four books of poetry: *The Lightning Field*, winner of the 2002 FIELD Poetry Prize; *Through the Window*; *Chalkmarks on Stone*; and *Taken From the River*. Her poems have been translated into Chinese, as well as Turkish, and have been published in journals, including *AGNI, Chicago Review, The New Republic, The New Yorker* and more. A recipient of a National Endowment for the Arts Creative Writing Fellowship and a Pushcart Prize, Moldaw teaches at the University of Southern Maine's Stonecoast Low Residency MFA Program.

- **Gina Ochsner** (Mainstream/Literary Fiction) won the Flannery O'Connor Award for Short Fiction for her first collection of stories, *The Necessary Grace to Fall* (University of Georgia). Her latest collection, *People I Wanted to Be*, was recently published by Houghton Mifflin.

- **Richard Peck** (Children's/Young Adult Fiction) is the first children's writer to receive a National Humanities Medal. He won the 2001 John Newberry Gold Medal for his 30th book, *A Year Down Yonder*. His 2003 book *The River Between Us* won the Scott O'Dell award in historical fiction. He's written a collection of short stories, *Past Perfect, Present Tense*, and the novel *The Teacher's Funeral* (all Dial Books).

- **Heather Sellers** (Memoir/Personal Essay) has taught nonfiction writing for 15 years. Her book *Page After Page* (Writer's Digest Books) assists writers at all levels with their writing practice. She's the author of four other books and recently completed her memoir, *Face First*.

We'd also like to acknowledge our first-round judges, who evaluated more than 18,000 entries: **Liza N. Burby** (Children's /Young Adult Fiction), **Ann Byle** (Inspirational), **Jim Cummins** (Rhyming Poetry), **Chad Gervich** (Television/Movie Script), **Marnie Hayutin** (Feature Article), **Debby Mayne** (Mainstream/Literary Fiction), **Miriam Sagan** (Non-rhyming Poetry), **Aury Wallington** (Stage Play), **Julie Wheeler** (Genre Short Story) and **David Vann** (Memoir/Personal Essay).

Finally, our most heartfelt congratulations to the winners and the entrants in this year's competition. The quality of your entries makes the judging more difficult each year. We look forward to seeing your work in the 76th Annual *Writer's Digest* Writing Competition Collection.

TABLE OF CONTENTS

HOUSE ON FIRE

Mary Feuer
Los Angeles, CA

The beauty of a house on fire can't be measured; the beauty of a house on fire is absolute. It's in the way the floors and walls cave in, the way the beams of the ceiling drop, all into the center, down to rubble and uncertainty, into air and ash. It's stunning.

I'm off duty now, but that doesn't matter. I pull my Ford Explorer past the barricade and I'm flagged down right away by a cop, who signals me to turn around. He holds a scarf over his nose and mouth with one hand; when I roll down my window it stings my eyes. There's a smell like new chimneys and the faint pungence of skunk.

"Lieutenant Bill Barnes. Station forty six, out of Wentworth," I tell the cop, pulling out my badge. He nods.

"It's gonna be a long night," he says as he waves me through. The sky glows red from flames and spinning truck lights, reflecting off the floating ash like excitement in the air.

I'll tell you something you may not know: a firefighter and a firestarter are two men in love with the same woman. They court her differently, one giving her everything she wants, the other fighting for control. Both love with equal passion. If I weren't on the Department, I don't even want to think about the things I'd have done by now.

My father had the same fascination. He could pick up the slightest whiff of embers in the air, could tell a pillar of smoke from a factory smokestack even from miles away. Family roadtrips were sidetracked. It didn't matter where we were headed—we would pull off the highway, following the scent, until we landed in front of the fire. It was his gift to me, this love. This devotion. By the time I was a teenager I'd watched at least thirty buildings burn down. We didn't talk about the losses, the people who died; I don't know how many there were. I do know that by then fire had already laid claim to my father, had begun the long years of toying with him the way a full cat torments a bird.

I steer the Explorer along the manicured road, into one of those communities whose new construction announces prosperity. Avenues and terraces with names of flowers, lined with rows of mock colonial housing, placed evenly and perfectly at regular intervals on spacious lots, the kind of home that says the man is providing. The houses contain the same blueprint, the same skeleton, but the differences in siding, shutters, patios, swingsets, give each a thin skin of individuality.

4

Inside the homes, coursing through them like corpuscles, are sons and daughters, mothers and fathers, so alike, yet pulsing with so much difference among them that many of these homes will explode before long. I used to have a house like this myself; my former wife still lives in it, alone now that our son is grown and gone.

The house I grew up in was a real colonial, two hundred years old, upright and narrow, crowded on either side by newer duplexes built barely four feet from the edge of our tiny lot. The word "neighborhood" still had meaning then: no shrubs separated us, no sprawling lawns to wave hello across. We were a tangle of arteries, on top of each other. If one house ignited, the entire block would have burned.

I remember a night when my father kicked at the frame of my bed to shake me awake. I must have been ten. I rolled over, rubbing my eyes, and there he stood, smiling, excited, my mittens and boots in his hand.

"Wanna go to a fire?" he said. I always did.

As we snuck past my parents' room I saw my mother, sound asleep. I'd never seen her that way before, all innocent and open, a feather of air all that came from her mouth. It was two a.m., only a few hours from her morning rosary, which she typically said at four thirty. I knew this not because I was normally up at the hour, but because I'd awakened once, and, looking for comfort from a bad dream, come upon her sitting in her rocking chair, mumbling, beads in hand. She was so livid at the interruption she spanked me ten times for every bead on the rosary, reddening my ass with Our Fathers, Glory Be's, and Hail Marys. Mary was my mother's name, too, but I was not the son she'd hoped I'd be. It seemed at the time I belonged to my father, despite her best efforts to make me her own.

My father and I slid quietly out the door, into the crisp New England chill. We could taste the burning wood as soon as we'd left the house, even though the fire was a good six blocks away, and the two of us barely spoke as we walked, breathing it in like peace. The two day old snow made a hefty crunch beneath our feet.

From the sidewalk we could see only thick smoke, no flames. The house was a two-story wooden saltbox on North Street. It had gone up suddenly. The single mother who lived there had three children who went to my school. I didn't know their names, barely their faces, but I saw only two of them on the street in their pajamas, clinging to their mother, the whole family wailing. A firefighter held the woman back; every sinew of her body demanded that she bolt into the burning house. As I watched her, in her anguish, I tried to imagine my own mother, shoeless in thin cotton on the street, sobbing for me, risking it all to save me. I couldn't picture it; the nearest I could get was her singing "Toora Loora Loora" with a rolling pin in her hand.

That was the first time I saw my father work. Normally when he had me with him he was a spectator, watching the on-duty men from the sidelines, speculating on strategy the way people do at high school football games. But the fire was growing, threatening the tight neighborhood. Demanding to be fed more men. Someone had some extra gear, so my father went behind the truck and grabbed a coat, a helmet. A pair of giant boots. In those days most of the guys used no breathing apparatus. The masks then were heavy and uncomfortable, plus it was a point of manly pride. My father rubbed my hair.

"For luck," he said. Then he went on in.

I stood on the sidewalk alone for maybe thirty minutes, watching the men climb the ladders that extended up off the trucks and aim the enormous hoses. Watching smoke pour out from where the front door used to be. Wondering where my father was.

Then I saw him, leaning on his axe handle, in an upstairs window. He took off his helmet and did what I'd seen other men in his squad do before when smoke overwhelmed them: he put his head out the window and threw up. After only seconds he wiped his mouth, replaced the helmet, pulled the collar of his coat up and disappeared back into the black smoke. It was then I knew I wanted this. I never thought about spending my life on anything else.

I'm careful not to drive over the engorged hoses as I pull the Explorer over. I open the back hatch and pull out my little video camera, my heavy coat. If I end up going in I'll have to come back for my gear. I see a few licks of orange snapping in the sky on the next block. I head on foot toward the center of my universe.

My parents had an understanding about this kind of thing. Not so my wife and I. Liz was quiet, unflamboyant, compassionate toward all living things almost to a fault. My mother, Mary, on the other hand, was the one the other parents on the block came to when the cute baby chicks they'd given their children at Easter had grown into chickens and roosters. We weren't farm people; killing was not required in our lives. But my mother would excitedly and swiftly execute the birds, chopping their heads off and watching their bodies run a few more steps before they realized they were dead. This fascinated her.

"The wonders God made," she'd say, amazed at their frantic movements. She herself was dead by the time I met Liz, gone to her beloved Jesus. When I told Liz what my mother did to the chickens, she wept for me.

Before she was my wife, Liz saw my devotion to the job as noble, selfless. She thought what I was obsessed with was the saving of lives and property. It's an easy misunderstanding, one many of us who walk this line encourage, because it's easier to explain: it makes us heroes. And we are heroes, that's the thing, heroics being the by-product of a certain darkness, a certain enslavement at the level of soul. Liz could never have understood this. Even the dark mystery of Catholicism was too much for her. She was a cultural Christian of the spiritual-but-not-religious variety. She went to Unitarian church each Easter. What did she know about destruction and resurrection? How could she know what it felt like to burn? Not that I'm a churchgoer. I'm not even a believer anymore. But I slept every night of my childhood below a portrait of Christ, his fiery, sacred heart blazing. That heart enters your body, just slides in through your nostrils and ears, until it more than haunts your dreams. It is your dreams.

Liz was five months pregnant with our son when she got her first real glimpse. She was craving ice cream, so we drove downtown to get cones. On the way back a sudden scent crossed the air, a fertile, charred scent, and I knew.

"This will only take a minute," I said, and smiled, and patted her hand. She smiled back, indulgent, as I turned the car down a side street, following the smell, and when we rounded the corner: a fully involved four-alarmer, an eight-unit dwelling, now a blaze that lit the block. I got out of the car as if sleepwalking, forgetting completely that I even had a wife.

When I returned to the car an hour later, the set of her eyes had reshaped. She'd been watching the families who lived in the apartments of the house, watching them sift through falling debris looking for beloved objects, watching them cry for everything they'd lost. I tried to turn the corners of my mouth down, but I was high on the smell of embers and my grin didn't want to be squelched. I looked at Liz; she looked at me. I could tell she knew: she saw me holding chickens down for my mother, fascinated with the wonder of life leaking out, chasing their headless forms around the yard. I was my mother's child after all.

There are two ladders here, and a rescue company. Three engines, one from my station, one from another house in Wentworth, and one from the neighboring town. I see Steve Gallagher, radio in hand, pacing.

"Hey, Deputy," I greet him. I've known him since high school. At the bar he's just Steve, but here I stick to formalities: he's the Incident Commander, after all. I wouldn't want to be Deputy Chief, not in a million years. He hardly ever gets to go into the fire.

My father was a Captain; we named my son after him, and called him Jimmy when he was small, but he started calling himself Jay in fourth grade. He's twenty-four now, just a year or so younger than I was when he was born. In all his life Jay's only been to two fires. When Liz and I were still married she said it wasn't healthy for a child.

"All boys love fires," I reasoned. "I went to fires as a kid and I turned out okay." We were in what would be the last year of our marriage.

"You turned out okay? That's funny," she said. By then, the edges of all of her words were razors. She would tell you, whether you asked her or not, that I was drinking too much then. Another thing she never understood. Whiskey is to the Irish what wine is to the Italians. In my house growing up, it flowed like milk.

Our arrangement gave me custody on the weekends. I moved out of our house, of course, to the one bedroom condo where I still live now. I put a dresser next to the sofa for Jay. He lived on the couch anyway, watching TV and playing video games.

When Jay was twelve, on a custody night, I heard a two-alarm brush fire on the scanner after dinner.

"Let's go," I said. Jay shrugged as if nothing mattered and got in the car with me. We drove to the blaze, one town over. I proudly showed my badge, my all-access backstage pass, and got us right up close.

We stayed there for about forty-five minutes. I had the big VHS camera back then, and got some incredible footage of a massive tree falling, burning leaves flying off of it like shooting stars, and of the new quint truck being broken in. Aaron Davis from Ladder fifty-two was pulled out on a stretcher. Jay wandered off fifteen minutes in. He came back smelling of cigarettes. He must have thought I wouldn't be able to tell because there was so much smoke in the air, but I remembered that combination from my father.

"I'm cold," said Jay. "This is retarded. You're shooting videos like it's a birthday party or something."

He said it loud enough for Aaron, on his stretcher in an oxygen mask, to hear. He looked up sharply at Jay, then at me. I grabbed Jay's arm and dragged him to the car. We were halfway home before I calmed down enough to ask him why he'd said that.

"It's stupid, the way you watch that stuff," he said. "It's like you're in love with someone who wants to kill you."

It is like that. Still, I'm glad my father never heard him say it. He was gone by then, dead from emphysema. From the smoke that more or less constantly filled his lungs.

I ask Deputy Chief Gallagher to fill me in.

"We've got four lines going," he says. "Got a ladder up out back. Joe Conroy's down, overcome by smoke. We're making progress but it's not contained, not by a longshot."

"If you need seconds, don't forget about me," I tell him. "I've got my gear in the car."

"Thanks, Bill, good to hear. I'll let you know," he says. But I doubt he'll send me in. Steve's one of the regular guys. He worries about my kind. Most of the firefighters nowadays, they don't have this kind of passion anymore. They just do the job and go home. Me, I'm tingling just to be this close. On the other side of this line of trucks is the house.

When Jay's trouble started I blamed Liz at first. He lived with her, mostly. They didn't get along. She couldn't control him. When, in his senior year of high school, he asked to move in with me full time, I can't say it didn't make me smug.

At first it was the just the kind of stuff high school kids do, drinking beers down at the lake and speeding home on dark, woodsy lanes with the headlights off for thrills. He was seventeen when he was got his first DUI. I pulled some strings with friends on the force and got the charge reduced to Reckless Operation. The second time, it wasn't so easy. Or the third: shortly after high school graduation he served a mandatory sixty days.

Not long after Jay got out of jail, I found a tobacco tin in his top drawer, beneath the underwear. I'd found his marijuana before; I'd smoked it before, to tell the absolute truth. I saw the weed and liquor as youthful indiscretion, innocent. But there was something else in the tin, a white substance I assumed then was cocaine.

"I can't believe you looked in my drawer!" Jay yelled. "What's all that bullshit you say about trust?"

"I'm your father. It's my house," I flailed, knowing that wasn't the thing to say, no idea what the thing to say was.

"Fuck that!" He hollered, "Fuck you!"

I hit him before I even knew I'd done it; my fist flew out as fast and hard as a blast of hydrant water. He looked stunned for a second, disbelieving, then, before I could move, he lunged at me.

I'm not proud of how it ended. We charged each other, gored bulls. Pure hate coursed through me; judging from the pummeling I took he felt the same way. Finally I landed a blow to his nose hard enough to break it; a heavy red trickle ran down his lip. He lurched back, reeled, fell on his ass. I win, the adrenaline told me, until I remembered he was my son.

Jay stormed off and didn't come home for a few days. By the time he did, I guess I'd given up. As he gathered his belongings, emptying the drawers I'd rifled, I didn't try to convince him to stay. I read the paper. I looked away.

"I'm moving in with some friends," he muttered on his way out the door. After that, neither his mother nor I even knew where he lived.

I tried to talk to Liz sometimes about Jay, but all she could say was, "Well? What do you expect?" As if it were my fault, as if I carried some gene, like I'd passed on some dangerous predilection. All the gentleness, the compassion had been drained from her, at least when she was speaking to me.

Jay came by the station house every now and then, when he needed money. Sometimes I gave it to him, depending how rough he looked. He was a handsome kid, and cleaned up well when he wanted to. Still, he couldn't seem to get a job.

"Take the fire exam!" I encouraged him once, after a dinner he shared with my crew.

He guffawed. "You're kidding, right?"

"It might be good for you. Give you someplace to put all that energy." Jay was so antsy you'd have thought he had some sort of disorder. He couldn't sit, jiggled his legs, ran his hand continuously through his hair. When he saw me pull out a twenty he said he'd think about it.

Later that night we got called in as back-up on a house fire in the seedy little neighborhood next to the warehouses, down by the tracks. By the time my truck arrived, the fire was contained, but still a thick smell of solvent hung in the air.

Clearly there'd been an explosion. The windows of the tiny white bungalow were blown out, charred black around the sills, but, weirdly, the shards of glass themselves were also completely black, as if they'd been painted that way. On the busted porch, a dirty stuffed bear suggested the presence of children, but there were no people, no one on the sidewalk looking anxiously toward home. Nobody there.

I went inside. A bottle of lye stood open on the grimy coffee table next to a half-eaten paper plate of french fries. There was litter everywhere, on every surface inside the two-room house, not rubble from the explosion, but the detritus of both family life and chemical processes: a pot caked with old macaroni and cheese, half a dozen empty bottles of drain cleaner, dirty diapers, jugs of chemicals, more toys, two hot plates, a baby bottle, a modified propane tank. When I saw all the torn packets of Sudafed and Revive, I knew I was looking at a homemade lab, for the cooking of crystal meth.

I was poking at the debris on the porch with the toe of my boot when I saw him. A disheveled figure striding purposefully up the walkway, twitching, knocking on the air as if it were a door. He was so turned inside out he didn't even notice the wrecked house, the fire trucks. Babbling unintelligibly to himself. Clutching twenty dollars. A madman with intensity and purpose. He took the front steps two at a time, almost walking right into me. It was Jay.

When he finally looked up, his eyes widened, but there was uncertainty in them, as if he were trying to figure out where he'd seen me before. His grinding jaw dropped when he finally saw the trashed house behind me, firefighters crossing in and out.

"No no no no," was what Jay said. "I was just here. No way."

I saw a cruiser at the end of the street, coming toward the house. "Go. Get out of here. Run," I hissed at him.

Jay stood in his confusion for a second or two. Behind him, the police were pulling up. He swung his head toward the cop car for a beat, looked back at me, open-mouthed, trying to find some words, then gave up and dashed off.

That's how I picture him whenever I think of him now: shielding his dilated eyes from the lights flashing red and blue, grasping for an excuse, finding none, backing up and running away. That was Jay's second fire.

I turn the corner, and the air is thick with heat. There she is: a wall, a tower, an avalanche of flames. So much power, so much consuming beauty. So much. I'm never prepared for it, never. My mind goes awestruck and overwhelmed every time. And it's never the same twice. No two houses burn the same way. I've seen siding melt. I've seen staircases stand when all else is consumed. I've seen houses intact on the outside, completely hollow, black, inside, and I've seen furniture preserved, pictures still hanging on walls above floors that are completely gone.

This ranch house has been ablaze for a little less than an hour; it's too early to guess how far it'll go. Already the roof looks weak in the front. Maybe a candle like the ones Liz loves to light started this; or a woman forgetting there's a loaf of bread in the oven, as I saw my mother do once. Maybe a stray match thrown down by a weary husband on the porch, or someone falling asleep on the couch with a cigarette going, the way Jay used to when he lived with me, though I don't think Jay sleeps much anymore.

I've told you I'm not a believer these days. But that's not entirely true. Standing here, at the altar of this burning house, prayers my mother taught me bubble up. And the names of our Patron Saints: Saint Florian, Patron Saint of firefighters. Saint Maximillian Kolbe, Patron Saint of addicts. Bernardine, protector of the lungs. Brigid, the Patron Saint of chickens. And Jude, of course, Jude, Patron Saint of lost causes, of which this house is one, of which my son is one. But most of all, Mary, Patron of all Mothers, pray for us sinners, now and at the hour of our death. Amen.

I aim the camcorder just in time to catch the roof as it caves in, displacing everything below it, sending spires of smoke and sparks shooting up. I have fallen like that. I've felt the floor drop out. The sky lights up like the Fourth of July and the air is charred and I breathe deeply, knowing I'm home.

SPRING SNOW

Alice Anne Ellis
Richmond, VA

Crystal fumbled in her haste to get the baby ready before Martha came home. Any minute now the rusty Oldsmobile would scrape into the driveway and Martha would hustle through the door, a bundle of shopping bags in her arms and a bundle of instructions in her mouth.

It was not that Crystal really minded all the instructions, the advice, the chores. After all, she, JD and the baby were living under Martha and Benjamin's roof. They could be expected to do their share. It was just that she felt she could never live up to Martha's expectations. She was cut out for failure, no matter what she did.

"Time you got Mercy washed and put to bed," Martha would say, setting her pile of groceries in the kitchen. Babies must have a "bedtime routine" in Martha's world. Or "I see you finished tidying those kitchen cabinets. The bathroom ones are next on the list, sugar-pie." Or "Sweetie, did you do the washing/mending/dusting/vegetables? You know Poppa's gonna want his ironed shirt/clean study/dinner ready when he gets in."

Sometimes Crystal felt like Cinderella, wielding the broom disconsolately round the kitchen floor, her long blonde hair lank and sad in sympathy with her situation. But Martha's not wicked, she would try to remind herself. And she's not my step-mother, she's my mother-in-law. And I do owe her and Benjamin something. JD and I both do.

But JD is their son, the Cinderella in her would whine in response. They'll look after him anyway. This is his house as much as theirs.

They are kind to me, though. They've given us and the baby a home. Do you think for one minute that Martha is going to let that baby out of her control? (Cinderella could get quite nasty.)

Martha loves Mercy, Crystal would argue with her Cinderella side. She just wants to give her the best.

Mmmphm, Cinderella would grimace sarcastically and toss the broom into the closet and slam the door.

"Oh Lord," said Crystal out loud, as she struggled to put Mercy into the fleece-lined suit that one of Martha's co-workers had given her. Mercy was about eleven months too small for it. "I'm going crazy in this house. We need to get out, don't we, Mercy? Do you know the last time I saw my friends? It was before you were born!"

Since she had been on homebound instruction there was seldom any reason to go to the school. Finding time to go to the public library to talk online was next to impossible. And what with Mercy's demands, Martha's restrictions and most of her friends having jobs, she had never managed to arrange meeting anyone at the mall. She did talk to her close friends when her cell phone was working but that wasn't often. Somehow, in the never-ending cycle of feeding, changing and washing, she kept forgetting to charge it. Then her account ran out of minutes and she couldn't go to the shopping center for several days to replenish it. And Martha didn't like Crystal using the house phone too much. She was mistrustful of the phone company's billing policy and followed the principle that the less it was used, the less likely it was that they would overcharge her. Crystal had made JD explain the phone bill to his mother more than once but it had done no good. Martha had her own ideas.

Crystal told all this to Mercy in her mind. The baby was growing fretful. One arm, small enough to escape easily from the sleeve of the suit, had wormed its way out of the neck. And even Mercy, at five weeks old, could tell this wasn't right—one arm in, one arm out.

"It's alright, sweetpea. We're going out to have some fun at last. I'll give you your bottle at the mall. Yes, Mercy! It's out to the mall, cradle and all!"

With luck she would see somebody there. A couple of people she knew worked in the food court. And some friends always used to hang out there after school.

The gravel crunched its complaint under the Oldsmobile but the sound was more distant than usual. Crystal lifted a corner of lace curtain and saw an inch of snow muffling the ground.

"That's OK. Looks like it's stopping. Won't give the Firebird any trouble." She looked at the tired blue Pinto outside the gate. JD had started calling it the Firebird after the first time they had sex in it. "Burns up the road!" he'd say, and he and Crystal would exchange a private look. That was in the early days.

A shadow passed the window. The next moment the front door opened and in came Martha, an orchestra of crackling bags, exclamations and cackling laughter.

"Ho my, it's cold out there! How's my sweet baby today? She been good? I swear, that traffic gets worse." Her voice receded into the kitchen.

Crystal quietly put on her coat. Mercy lay on the sofa, one arm still flailing free of her suit. Martha's voice came closer again but stopped in mid-sentence at the living room door.

"Crystal, honey, where you think you're going with Mercy in this weather?"

"The mall." Crystal started wrestling Mercy's waving arm into her padded suit.

"Crystal, it's freezing out there. I don't even think you should drive, hon. The roads are getting slick."

"I'll be fine."

"Unh-uh, Crystal."

"Martha, I really need to get out. I'm going to meet some friends at the mall." Crystal gave up the struggle with Mercy's arm and zipped up the suit with the baby's arm inside, across her chest. Mercy's complaint became louder.

"You are not going anywhere, sweetie. You know the tires on that old Pinto are as bald as Mercy's bottom!"

"I'm only going to the mall," said Crystal, trying to keep her voice even, avoiding Martha's eye. She knew the authority in that glance could pinion her in a second. Keep moving, she told herself, and stomped to the hall closet for the baby's car seat.

When she came back, Martha was holding the baby on her shoulder, patting her gently and whispering into her neck. The fleecy suit lay in a pile on the sofa.

Rage washed through Crystal's mind like a tidal wave. I am going out, she wanted to scream. Give me MY baby. I'm going to get MY life back.

"Has she had her bottle yet?" Martha asked quietly.

Crystal's throat felt it would bleed from the sob she wouldn't let out.

"Unh-uh." The bottle was in the kitchen. Ready to take to the mall.

"Want to watch TV while you feed her?" asked Martha, still talking quietly and looking at the snow fall outside. Fat flakes drifted down, sparse but stubborn. "I'll make you some pancakes."

Against the snowy light from the window Martha's shape was like a rock, solid and immovable. Mercy squirmed, quieter now, on the shoulder of the rock.

"It's too cold for a tiny baby, hon."

Crystal honestly did not know what she would do. She had no thoughts any more. No logic, no intention.

Then she said, "Not too cold for me, though."

In one movement, like a hiss of steam, she was through the door, in the Pinto, skidding down the road.

[EXCERPT FROM A YOUNG ADULT NOVEL]

I THOUGHT MY INSURANCE COVERED THAT!

Christy Heitger-Casbon
Noblesville, IN

*The names and details in the stories depicted here have been changed, but the lesson of each story is real.

Here's a riddle for you: What's black and white, and gray all over? Answer: The details of your homeowner's insurance policy.

At least that's how it may seem when it comes time to file a claim. You thought your coverage was fairly clear, but it's only after misfortune befalls your property that you learn all about various exclusions and optional coverage.

So, what's a cabin owner to do? You've heard the phrase, "The best defense is a good offense?" That adage applies here. To avoid confusion, it's wise to consult your insurance agent before you experience some major cabin crisis. Doing so can save you a lot of headaches, irritation, and, best of all—money!

Hopefully you'll never have to deal with major calamities such as the ones in the following scenarios. But it doesn't hurt to educate yourself and be prepared. After all, isn't preparation what insurance is all about?

I thought my insurance covered...damage from a flood.

When the skies opened up during their evening campfire, Jen and Jeff Morgan didn't think much of it. They simply grabbed their s'mores and headed inside. But when the rain turned torrential and continued to pound their cabin, a flash flood ensued, and their deck washed away. Their first thought was, "Thank God for homeowner's insurance!"

But when they spoke to their insurance agent, they learned something they didn't know before: Water damage is typically covered under homeowner's insurance only if the cause of loss is due to water that is wind-borne. For example, if hurricane-force winds shattered your cabin's windows, allowing rain to blow in and soak your hard wood floors, insurance would pay.

Flood damage, on the other hand, is only covered by special insurance purchased through the Federal Emergency Management Agency (FEMA). A flood is defined as any situation where water is rising up from the surface. If a lake or stream overflows (even though it may be the result of a rainstorm) and enters your dwelling, that's flooding. Or if a levee breaks and water pours into your home, that's flooding. The freak rainstorm that demolished the Morgan's deck is also categorized as flooding because the heavy rains caused water to rise from the ground's surface.

Given that their cabin was nowhere near a moderate- or high-risk flood zone, the Morgans never considered purchasing separate flood insurance. But here's an interesting tidbit. According to Tully Lehman, spokesman for the Insurance Network of California, 25 percent of claims paid for flood damage are in areas that are considered low to moderate risk. Hmmm, something to think about.

I thought my insurance covered...the full value of my home and belongings.
Crash! Boom! On occasion, during heavy Midwestern thunderstorms, Liz and Randy Smith enjoyed listening to and watching the thunder and lightning from the safety of their cabin. One April night a real hum-dinger of a spring storm blew over the lake, and around 1 a.m. —Crack! Sploosh!— a tree fell and caved in, part of their roof, destroying not only their beautiful Persian area rug but the 32-inch television that sat in the corner of the room.

The following morning when the Smiths called their insurance agent, they were schooled in the difference between actual cash value and replacement cost. Actual cash value is the actual cash that the insurance company provides to replace a property minus any depreciation of the item based on its usage.

Replacement cost, on the other hand, pays the dollar amount needed to replace the damaged property without a deduction for depreciation.

"It's a difficult concept for many folks to comprehend because they see their property value appreciating each year and assume that means their cabin's structure is appreciating, as well," says Lehman. "In reality, however, the materials used to build your cabin are actually losing value as it ages due to wear and tear."

In the Smith's case, insurance paid a percentage value based on the roof's depreciation (i.e., the insurance company paid the actual cost value of the roof rather than the replacement cost). As for the Persian rug and the TV?

Well, the Smiths also got a crash course on two other similar terms: actual cash value for contents versus replacement cost coverage for contents. With actual case value for contents (which is what a typical policy offers unless you choose to upgrade), insurance provides coverage to purchase the item (in this case, a five-year-old, 32-inch television) minus the depreciation cost of that item (say, 25 percent of the original price of $500), resulting in a settlement of $375. Had the Smith's policy been previously upgraded to replacement cost coverage for contents, they could have headed to their local electronics store and purchased a brand new 32-inch television, and insurance would have paid for whatever it cost. This is because with replacement cost coverage the carrier pays the amount it would cost to buy the item in today's marketplace.

I thought my insurance covered...damage caused by freezing pipes.
It was early March and John Lazwik's family couldn't wait to spend spring break at their beloved northeastern cabin. When they stuck their key in the lock and swung open the door, however, their mouths hit the squishy floor. Much of their cabin and its contents were saturated, apparently due to pipes

that had frozen, burst, and then thawed.

It wasn't clear at first if insurance would pay. The claims examiner had to inspect the property to determine the cause of loss. What kind of shape were the pipes in? Had the Lazwiks performed routine maintenance to the pipes, checking periodically for water leakage and rust spots? (Note: If you're away from your cabin for extended periods of time, you may want to look into technologies such as temperature sensors that can monitor your piping system and detect various problems in your pipes including leaks or low pressure.)

(And another note if you're away from your cabin for weeks or months at a time: Check your policy for occupancy requirements. Some policies won't cover this type of damage if no one was in the dwelling within a specific time frame.)

Every carrier is different, but for the most part insurance companies pay for a certain number of circumstances termed "covered causes of loss." Even so, all "covered causes of loss" are subject to various exclusions, including, for instance, "intention of loss" (e.g., purposefully setting a fire to collect insurance money), or "wear and tear" (e.g., neglecting to perform normal upkeep to your pipes).

In the Lazwik's case, insurance paid for the damage because the Northeast had experienced record low temperatures that winter. However, when the claims examiner inspected the 25-year-old pipes, he found that some had rust spots, so he suggested the Lazwiks replace the old pipes, which they promptly did. It was a wise choice, not only to help prevent future disaster but also because if the same thing happened again anytime soon, insurance would likely cite negligence and not pay a cent.

"Insurance is made to cover events that you don't anticipate and can't keep from happening no matter what you do," explains Matthew Cullina, property team manager for product development with MetLife Insurance in Warwick, R.I. "Maintenance, however, is in your control."

Don't confuse an insurance policy with a household maintenance fund.

I thought my insurance covered...fire damage.

It was a beautiful, cool Southwestern evening, so Cecily Rudolph decided to create a cozy cabin atmosphere by burning some candles. She lit three buttercream votives and set them in the family room's windowsills, then headed to the kitchen to start dinner. A few moments later a breeze blew a corner of the curtain into the flame. Within minutes, the room was ablaze. Rudolph grabbed the fire extinguisher, and the neighbors came running to help, but it was too late. The family room was gutted.

Rudolph was devastated to lose the central and favorite room of her vintage, 900-square-foot cabin. Soon she received more devastating news. In the 45 years since her cabin had been erected, the county had dramatically changed its building codes. The new laws required that Rudolph demolish her cabin and rebuild it to meet the new zoning regulations and governmental safety standards. This included making the structural walls two inches thicker as well as building the cabin 50 feet farther back from the lake.

Typical property insurance would provide payment sufficient to cover only the damaged part of Rudolph's cabin (the family room). In contrast, ordinance or law coverage (optional coverage which typically is purchased separately) would provide any type of upgrade that is needed due to building code changes in the local community. Rudolph hadn't purchased this coverage because she didn't even know it existed. A lot of people don't understand why insurance won't pay for an upgrade that the government requires.

Property insurance contracts promise to restore your home to the way it was. But when the state, county, or local government steps in and says the way it was is not good enough today—well, that's not what the insurance company bargained for when it sold you the contract.

Although some high-end policies include ordinance or law coverage, most standard policies do not. In addition, ordinance or law coverage is a bigger issue in some locations than others. For instance, in states with high regulations like California (because of the threat of earthquakes), laws require new construction to meet extra measures of safety.

The best way to protect yourself is to ask your agent what type of ordinance or law coverage you have and whether you should buy additional coverage.

***

Go ahead and give your insurance agent a jingle. He or she can answer all of your questions.

And just for kicks you can share the following cabin riddle: What never goes bad, always looks good, and gets sweeter with age? Answer: your cabin, of course!

Freelancer Christy Heitger-Casbon's home once suffered water damage (and insurance paid!) when her washing machine malfunctioned.

A disclaimer: Policies among insurance carriers vary, and each claim is dependent on its own particular facts.

Help!
To help prevent some of the calamites depicted in this article, you may wish to check out these home protection services:
- Arctic Trace, electric heat trace,
  (907) 522-3004, www.arctictrace.com
- Heat-Line, electric heat trace,
  (800) 584-4944, www.heatline.com
- Protected Home, water and temperature monitor/alert system,
  (800) 880-6000, www.protectedhome.com
- Sensaphone, early warning notification,
  (877) 373-2700, www.sensaphone.com
- Talking Thermostats.com,
  (800) 838-8860, www.talkingthermostats.com

BAD WITCH

Rachael M. Haring
Cliffwood, NJ

Alicia strode across the lobby of Daimon Technologies, unobtrusively glancing at her reflection in the mirrored wall. She liked what she saw: snakeskin Prada shoes, tight black skirt-suit, porcelain skin, chestnut hair long and straight. She looked powerful. She looked ready for anything.

The security desk chirped its recognition as she approached, and the receptionist gave her a polite smile.

"Good morning, Miss."

Alicia regarded him coolly, her thoughts taking carnal turns. He was an appealing specimen: young, blond, and vapidly pleasant, probably an NYU undergraduate spending his summer in the field. His name badge said "Thomas."

"Good morning to you," she purred. She raised an eyebrow. "You're new. Enjoying yourself?"

She noticed his gaze dip towards her cleavage and then quickly slide back to her face.

"Yes, of course," he responded with a nervous smile.

"Good," she replied. She brushed her fingertips against his arm. *My office*, she mentally suggested. *Seven o'clock. Come alone.*

The boy blinked, but his expression didn't change. Alicia gave him a small, knowing smile and walked away.

He'd obey. They always did.

Alicia swept through the silver corridor, granting nods to some of the more important people she passed. The first spell of the day always felt so good. Forget caffeine: this was the ultimate awakening, the ultimate morning rush.

Alicia saw her office at the end of the corridor, and by the door, her new assistant's cubicle. Kiera sat statue-still, staring intently at her computer screen; as Alicia approached, her head jerked up.

"Oh, Ms. Carman! Good morning! I ... er ... started a pot of coffee, if you'd like some ..."

"Only tea," Alicia said. She walked past the girl and tapped the keypad by her office door. "Chamomile with lemon."

"Of course," Kiera agreed. "I'll get you some right away."

"You do that," Alicia replied. She looked at the girl's reflection in the dark glass of her door. "Then bring me the file on Charles Peterson."

Without waiting for an answer, Alicia strode into the quiet cool of her office. She tossed her briefcase on the desk, then leisurely walked to the floor-to-ceiling window and twirled open the blinds. Manhattan spread before her, sparkling in the morning sunlight. She never tired of taking in this view. The city was an urban kingdom of never-ending traffic, towering billboards, and glass and steel monoliths. And at last, here she was, where she belonged: high above everything, in her own personal Olympus.

Alicia smirked as she thought of the office's former tenant. Poor, forgotten Ms. Nichols. She had never taken the time to enjoy this heavenly view. She had been the top negotiator at Daimon, driven and relentless, embedded into her profession like a tick into flesh—or at least she had been until Alicia joined the team. But then, gradually, as if a dark spirit whispered into her ear, Ms. Nichols began to realize the worthlessness of her life. She began to see that no matter how hard she worked, no matter how high she rose, she'd never get anywhere. There was no point in struggling.

It was better to just ... *disappear*.

And so, one rainy Tuesday commute, Ms. Nichols threw herself in front of the A line. The trains were shut down for hours as they cleaned her off of the rails.

Her co-workers wondered why she had done it. But Alicia didn't wonder. She knew. She knew every doubting voice in Ms. Nichols's head, every suicidal thought, every dark suggestion. And why wouldn't she? She had put them all there herself.

Behind her, the door creaked, and there was a clink of ceramic on wood.

"Your tea, Ms. Carman. And the file."

Alicia raised her hand and silently dismissed the girl.

Let's see what we have here, she thought, paging through the file. Charles Peterson, Chief Technological Officer, Adapa Corporation. Interested in several Daimon products, including the new multi-database integration program ...

Alicia took a swig of her tea, wincing at the excess of lemon. Daimon Tech would do quite well on this. She flipped through the rest of the file, idly practicing her casting gestures with her left hand. The motions were nearly second nature: her fingers effortlessly curved and bent into the mystic positions. There was no thought, only will.

Eventually, the intercom on her desk buzzed.

"Ms. Carman?" came Kiera's tentative voice. "Mr. Peterson is here for your 9:00. Shall I send him to room A-2?"

Languidly, Alicia depressed the reply button.

"Yes. I'll be there."

***

Alicia took her time getting to A-2. When she finally entered, she found a portly, balding man sitting at the head of the table. A startling array of charts and contracts spread before him like a colorful, statistics-themed tablecloth. He seemed slightly nervous, she noted with satisfaction.

Peterson rose and extended his hand. "Good morning. You must be Ms. Carman."

"Yes, hello, Mr. Peterson. I was just reading up on your company." As she withdrew her hand, she curled her fingers in a subtle magic sign. "Twenty corporate offices, if I'm not mistaken?"

He nodded. Deep in his eyes, she could see the charm start to take effect.

"Yes ... exactly. And we'd like to use your software to tie them all together."

Alicia nodded. "Well, have a seat, Mr. Peterson, and we'll see what we can do."

An hour later, Peterson signed Alicia's pre-made contract with a pleased smile. He imagined that his ideas had been his alone, that his choices were sound. The delusion would last as long as she wanted it to. And if anyone at his organization doubted or challenged him, well ... Alicia had learned long ago that people were remarkably adept at molding current attitudes to fit past decisions. She hadn't lost a contract yet.

"Thank you, Ms. Carman," Petersen said as they both gathered their papers and rose to their feet. "I think both of us will benefit from this agreement."

Alicia turned to the door.

"See my assistant on your way out. She'll arrange payment."

Thomas stood beside Alicia's desk, self-consciously buttoning his khakis.

"So ... do you want to go get a drink?" he asked. He finished dressing and glanced up at her. "I know this great bar just a—"

"No, I don't think so," Alicia interrupted smoothly. She crossed her legs and latticed her hands behind her head. "I'm going to stay here and finish a few things. And you're going to leave."

He paused, looking vaguely lost. She would have pitied him, had she not been so utterly amused by his powerlessness.

"Oh ... sure," he finally said. "I just thought maybe we could ..."

"There isn't any 'we,' Thomas," Alicia replied with a small chuckle. "Don't misunderstand: I enjoyed your company very much. But now you ought to go home. Quietly."

He swallowed. Behind her head, Alicia bent her fingers into a very precise emotional evocation. She summoned embarrassment, uncertainty, fear ...

You can't tell anyone what you did tonight, Thomas, she mentally warned. *Never let them know.*

His head moved in a tiny, almost involuntary nod. Slowly, as if he were walking in his sleep, he shrugged his coat over his shoulders and left the office.

"See you Friday," Alicia smiled as the door clicked closed.

She released a careless sigh and buttoned her blouse. Thomas had been a pleasant diversion, but now, it was time to catch up on a few work-related issues. Most notably, she needed to prepare for the impending visit from Peabody Systems. They were sending their top negotiator to Daimon on Friday morning, a man called Jens Dane. Alicia had never met this Mr. Dane, but she had heard others talking about him with awe in their voices. His reputation was wide-spread, it seemed.

Alicia snorted. Well, no matter how good he was, he had no hope of defeating a witch. Let him try his games and compliments: in the end, she'd get what she wanted. She always did.

Her computer had long gone to sleep, and Alicia jiggled the mouse. As color returned to her screen, she noticed that her e-mail icon flashed with a new message.

We Know, said the subject line, but the sender was blank. Alicia sighed. It was probably yet another spam promising to enlarge body parts she didn't even have. Still, an odd pique of curiosity drove her to open the message.

You haven't followed the rules. For that, you'll suffer what you've spread.
—The Benevolence

Alicia frowned, re-reading the message. What in the world was that supposed to mean? It had to be a prank, or a mistake, or some sort of new and annoying advertising. It didn't even have her name on it.

Without a second thought, she deleted it.

But early the next morning, when she opened her e-mail, she saw the same message.

You'll suffer what you've spread.

Briefly, Alicia considered calling the tech department and asking them where this thing had come from, but she quickly squashed the idea. She could handle this. It was just random nonsense, the price to pay for living in the age of the internet. It was nothing to get upset about.

After lunch, the message reappeared. And again, the next morning, this time with a slight variation.

Alicia Anne Carman, it said at the top.

So, they knew her after all. Alicia's eyes drifted over the last words, and the tiniest glimmer of recognition stirred in the very back of her mind ...

The Benevolence. It sounded familiar, but she couldn't quite discern why. Had she heard of them before? How had they—

"Ms. Carman?" said a soft voice, startling Alicia from her paranoid thoughts. She emitted an undignified yelp and turned to see her assistant standing in the doorway.

"Yes? What do you want?" Alicia snapped.

Kiera lowered her eyes and placed a bundle of papers on the edge of the desk.

"I'm sorry, Ms. Carman. I just wanted to bring your mail."

Alicia released a short sigh. "All right. Now leave me alone."

Kiera obeyed, and Alicia flipped through the stack of letters. At the bottom of the pile, there was a thin, crimson envelope, addressed to her in flowing letters. A wax seal marked the back of the envelope: a grinning skull encircled with branches.

Let me guess, she thought to herself, swallowing hard. *Not a party invitation.*

Inside, a card bore another message.

It's all coming back to you, Alicia. Bad witches get what they deserve.
—*The Benevolence*

***

More mysterious e-mails arrived on Thursday. Alicia didn't bother opening any of them: she simply deleted the messages, busily assuring herself that they meant nothing at all.

Most likely, this was some sort of sick joke amongst the junior negotiators. Alicia had made a few enemies on her way to the top of the department, and it wouldn't surprise her if they called her a witch behind her back. As long as she didn't show them how it bothered her, this stupid game would stop.

Alicia arrived at her office early Friday morning to find her mail already resting on the corner of her desk. Though her throat tightened with anticipation and her fingers shook as she went through the letters, there was no crimson letter to be found. Likewise, there was nothing of note in her e-mail inbox.

Alicia leaned back in her chair with a short sigh. Finally, this silliness was over. And not a moment too soon: today was the meeting with Dane, and she needed to be completely focused, completely confident. Alicia had already decided to clear out Dane's entire technology budget for the year: nothing less would be a victory.

Alicia called her assistant into the office.

"Yes, Ms. Carman?"

"Kiera, I want a record of the negotiations this morning. You're to take steno."

"Of course, Ms. Carman," the girl nodded jerkily, hands clasped behind her back like an attentive schoolgirl. "This is the meeting with Mr. Dane of Peabody, correct?"

A faint swirl of anxiety moved in Alicia's guts, an uncharacteristic emotion, and she consciously steeled herself against it. It wasn't like her to fear anyone, let alone a fellow negotiator.

Alicia gathered the files from her desk, and swept out of the office.

"Let's go."

***

Dane was a typical icy-eyed Scandinavian with hair the color of summer wheat and a chiseled, unreadable countenance. He was younger than Alicia had expected, and undeniably handsome; when she entered the conference room, he rose to his feet and gave her a wide smile.

"Why, hello, Ms. Carman." He leaned closer, his expression turning playfully conspiratorial. "It's good to finally meet you. You have quite a fearsome reputation among your colleagues."

Alicia accepted his handshake.

"As do you, Mr. Dane," she replied easily. She swept her hand toward the table. "Shall we? We have much to discuss."

Alicia sat across from her opponent, and Kiera silently sequestered herself at the end of the table.

"So," Alicia began, determined to grasp control, "I understand that your company is looking at several of Daimon's most innovative technologies."

"Yes, indeed," Dane replied, nodding sagely. "But I must warn you now: 'looking' is the operative word here. At this point, we're not committed to anyone." He spread his hands on the table and summoned another charming smile. "That's why I'm here, Ms. Carman. I need to know what kind of a partner Daimon would be."

Alicia adjusted her glasses with her left hand; her right hand, however, performed a quick charm spell beneath the table's edge.

"Well, Mr. Dane," she said, "I see here that you've got quite a few world-wide locations to connect. Certainly, you'll want to license at least two hundred copies of Moneta per international building, and more for the—"

"Wait a moment, please," Dane interrupted politely. "Don't you think that's an awfully high number?"

Alicia looked up at him with surprise. He met her eyes evenly: she saw no trace of magic clouding his gaze, no hesitation on his face.

Again, her hand curved in a charm sign, more deliberate this time.

"I think you'll find it's necessary to ensure that all of your departments are covered," she said, but he shook his head.

"No, no, this is going to be on a trial basis, if anything at all." He smiled, charming and unaffected as ever. "No offense intended, of course. Daimon is a quality provider. It's just not the *only* provider."

Alicia could feel her face warming with fury and humiliation. Why wasn't her magic working? How was he resisting her?

"In any case, Ms. Carman, let's not drag this out," Dane continued. He slid a small packet towards her. "I have here a list of locations we'd like to outfit with your Moneta program, along with the requested prices. There's not a whole lot to discuss, really. It only comes down to whether you're willing to do it."

Alicia stared at the paper and struggled to gather her wits. The prices were ridiculously low. She had to talk him into more. She couldn't lose her composure. She couldn't fail. Fear swirled through her blood like icy water.

"Mr. Dane," she said slowly, breathing a deep and calming breath, "I don't think you realize just how valuable Daimon Technologies can be to your organization."

Beneath the table, she tried the strongest charm-sign she knew. For a brief, shining moment, she thought she saw a shift in his expression; before she could continue, however, the lucid certainty returned to his eyes, and he shook his head.

"I understand completely," he returned. He leaned a little closer, tapped the list of prices he had given her, and smiled. "Now, do you understand what I'm saying, Ms. Carman?"

Despair and hatred clouded Alicia's thoughts. This wasn't the way it was supposed to be. She was supposed to be the one in control.

But somehow, the bastard knew that she had no choice. She had to get this contract, even if that meant submitting to his will.

"Fantastic, Ms. Carman," Dane gloated, shoving more papers under her nose. "Just sign here and here, and we'll get this partnership underway."

She did so, her mind awash in raging, mortified thoughts. Dane said his goodbyes, and Alicia merely sank back into her chair, staring at the wall.

"Ms. Carman, are you all right?" questioned a small, timid voice.

Kiera. She had almost forgotten that the girl was in the room. Lovely. Someone else to recognize her failure.

"Yes," she responded hoarsely.

Kiera looked uncertain, but she nonetheless stood and moved towards the door.

"I'll go type up the notes, then," she offered lamely. The door clicked closed.

Slowly, Alicia rose to her feet. She slid the new contract in her file and pulled its tie closed; as she did so, she saw a slip of paper resting where Dane had been sitting, its edges ragged and torn.

She turned it over and read the scribbled text.

Bad witches get what they deserve.

***

Alicia didn't leave her apartment all weekend.

Instead, she sat at her computer, hunched and dry-eyed, searching for more information on Jens Dane. She crawled the internet, read articles he had done for the negotiators' association, and e-mailed a few of her contacts, but by Sunday night, she had found nothing out of the ordinary. He was a respected businessperson, a member of several associations, and an author of three books on personal leadership.

What's your secret, you tricky, blonde bastard? I know you did something to me. I know you did.

Alicia lay in bed early Monday morning, her mind halfway between dream and recollection. She remembered the first time she had used The Will. It had been nearly a decade ago, but she still remembered how the warm, silversweet power had gushed through her thoughts, how her fingers had bent into its secret language of domination. The Will was her family's gift, given to her by her mother, entrusted to her and her alone. How could someone else take away that power? Could The Will be known to other families, other witches, or Goddess forbid, warlocks? Mother had never said anything about that.

Annoyance stirred in Alicia's half-formed thoughts. Not even a warning. Not even a hint. Useless crone.

The alarm chirped, and Alicia hauled herself out of bed. The higher-ups would want an explanation. They would want to know what had happened, and she would need The Will to satisfy them.

You have to fix this, she told herself as she dressed. *Stay calm. Remember your power. This can all be fixed.*

Her confidence grew during breakfast, flourished during her commute, and resounded in her mind as she strode through Daimon's lobby and gave Thomas a sly smile. She'd get another meeting with Dane and redouble her efforts, get him to change the contract. He couldn't beat her. She wouldn't let him.

But when Mr. Castle called her into his office for the inevitable inquiries, Alicia once again found that The Will had no effect. No matter how she curled her fingers behind her back, no matter how she pushed her mental voice into his mind, there was no response.

What's happening? This is ridiculous. How is Dane doing this? How ...

" ... was a bad deal, Alicia," dour old Castle was grumbling, as if she didn't already know. "Very bad. Obviously, your judgment is currently impaired. As of now, I'm taking you off of the SysTech accounts, as well as the upcoming meeting with Smythe and Sons."

Alicia wanted to protest, but her throat was too raw and tight for speech. Castle dismissed her, and she stalked into the hallway, her every muscle painfully clenched.

She couldn't believe it. Two of her largest accounts, gone.

Alicia swept into her office and rested her burning cheeks in her hands. Out of the corner of her eye, she saw the phone's light blinking.

A few button-stabs brought the message forward, where it vibrated through the large speaker on Alicia's phone.

"Hello, Ms. Carman. Jens Dane here. I just wanted to thank you for your benevolence in the meeting yesterday afternoon ..."

***

A knock sounded at the apartment door, yanking Alicia from her dark and listless dreams.

"Ms. Carman?" came a familiar, tentative voice. "It's me, Kiera."

Alicia groaned and rolled over on the couch, turning her face to the darkness. She tried to close her eyes and fall back into faceless slumber, but the damned girl wouldn't let her.

"Ms. Carman, please," Kiera said. "Let me in. I need to talk to you."

Alicia ached all over, and her mouth was foul and dry as rotting cotton; still, some strange impulse forced her to her feet and pushed her towards the voice. She leaned her forehead on the cool metal door and rested her fingers on the knob.

"What do you want?" she rasped.

The floor in the hallway creaked.

"Please, Ms. Carman, just let me come in."

With a great exhale, Alicia unlatched the door. What did it matter? So what if her assistant saw her hungover and miserable and wearing rumpled, two-day-old clothes? It wasn't as if Alicia commanded any respect around the office any more. Everyone thought she had crashed. And she had. Without her magic, she had nothing. Dane had taken it all from her, and she couldn't do a thing against the bastard.

Alicia slumped into a chair as Kiera entered. The girl looked frazzled and nervous as always, her hair tied into a wispy ponytail and her gloved hands clenched.

"Ms. Carman ... we're all worried. About you, I mean. You haven't been at the office for days."

Alicia slumped on the couch. "I'm sick."

Kiera paused uncertainly, then took a seat across from her.

"You seem more than sick, Ms. Carman," Kiera finally said. "You seem ruined. Like you have nothing left."

A wave of despair swept over Alicia's heart like dark water, shoving it downward, below the surface. "I ... don't ... "

Kiera leaned forward. "This demotion has devastated you."

Alicia wanted to turn away from the girl, wanted to return to faceless slumber, but she simply couldn't gather enough energy to move. Kiera's words were true, so painfully true ...

It's hopeless, Alicia mourned. Her throat constricted, and she swallowed the sob. *Utterly hopeless.*

Kiera rose and walked to the credenza separating Alicia's kitchen from the front room. She searched the cluttered surface and picked something thin and brassy from the low shelf.

"I wish I could say something that would help you," Kiera said honestly. She walked towards Alicia, her right hand glinting. "I wish I could tell you what needs to be done. But you've always been so good at figuring things out, Ms. Carman. Just hang in there, okay? You'll figure out what to do."

Dark compulsions stirred in the depths of Alicia's mind, like reflections in a pool of blood, and she tried to make sense of them. She had to do something. She had to get away from this pain, this worthlessness. She had to ... *disappear*.

Something moist and cold touched Alicia's palm, like a melting icicle against her skin. Blearily, she looked down. A simple, dagger-shaped letter opener rested in her hand. The compulsion grew stronger.

Disappear.

Trembling with resistance, Alicia placed the dagger's tip against her chest. A host of images filtered through her struggling thoughts: Kiera carrying the mail, Kiera sitting in the corner and quietly taking steno, Kiera smiling with obsequious cheer ...

"You," she whispered with dawning terror, but the presence in her mind expanded, easily subduing every other thought.

The Will has protectors, Alicia, it sang with Kiera's voice. *Watchers, and protectors, and judges. They know that you're a bad witch. And you know what happens to bad witches, don't you? Bad witches disappear.*

With a frightened, helpless whimper, Alicia shoved the blade into her chest.

STILL WATERS

Jan Ledford
Franklin, NC

That girl talks to Myrl Wells like she makes sense, and I despise her for it. 'She' being either one of them. Myrl on that reclining chair with the blanket they put on her legs, or that little deacon girl from the church. Everyone knows that girls can't be deacons, but that Baptist church downtown, the big one, must be hurting to elect girls in. Must be no men among 'em. But she talks to Myrl like either one of 'em has any sense.

Of course I stay out of it totally.

She came by today ... again. Lord, she was just here yesterday. Is there no rest for the weary? Me, I mean.

They'd had Myrl dressed for an hour or two I guess, and in that reclining chair. What's the point; bed or chair? They always park her in front of the window where she holds forth. With no one. Lord, that woman's rarely quiet. But she'd fallen asleep today, sometime between breakfast and lunch, and was bein' still at last. Until she intruded.

"I'm Jess, from your church, Mrs. Wells."

Myrl is obviously not awake.

"Mrs. Wells? Good morning. You having a little nap?"

Yes, she's asleep. Is that girl blind? The blind leading the blind. *I chuckle inside at my own Bible joke. Girls ought not to be deacons.*

"What...?" Myrl is rousing.

"It's Jess, Mrs. Wells. From the church. You were taking a little cat nap."

Jess is a man's name, everyone knows that. Maybe they voted her in by mistake, on the ballot.

"Oh."

"I came to see you. How are you doing today?"

"I'm alright, I guess ... "

Well, what is she supposed to say? 'I'm stuck here in this dad-blamed nursing home but it doesn't matter 'cause I'm seven-eighths out of my mind anyway'?

"Your blanket is on the floor. Do you want it on your legs?"

"No. I got hot. I'm hot today. This shirt is hot."

"I'll put it over here. Is that alright?"

Lord, neither one of them shuts up. Put the blasted blanket down and get on with the visit, since you're here. Again.

"Yeah."

"We didn't get our snow, did we?"

"Well, we did."

"No, look out the window. No snow out there today."

"Just a little. The children are playing in it."

"They're having fun, aren't they?"

I hate this worse than anything, when the little deacon girl goes along with Myrl's hallucinations. Like there are any kids outside. The nurses and aides here, they try to keep everyone grounded in reality. Today is Thursday, February 12. The weather is cold and cloudy. The next holiday is Valentine's Day. Lunch is tomato or potato soup and sandwiches. La, da, da.

"Oh, yes, but that little one, he's cute isn't he? I remember your baby. He was so cute."

"That's been a while back, Mrs. Wells!"

"But he was so cute, and they was coming over. I never went there before."

Didn't no such thing as Myrl know this girl's baby, even though I've only known Myrl since she's been my roommate for three months. You can tell by the way the girl talks, she's not from around here. May be a lot I don't know, but I do know that.

"I brought my Bible with me today. Can I read something to you?"

"If you want."

This is new; that girl never read anything before. To Myrl, I mean. Last week she sang "Do Lord." Not half bad, even if girls don't belong to be deacons. She could sing alright. Had a decent sense of rhythm, too.

"It's the 23rd Psalm. You know that, don't you?"

"Well, I don't know."

"Oh, I bet you do. I'll read it, and you say it with me..."

She reads the words.

And I say them along, in my mind.

They are beautiful, just like I remember, and lap at me like the gentle waters they describe.

Myrl must remember, too.

"You *do* know it." Jess's voice says she is pleased to make this connection with Myrl. "I saw you mouthing the words."

"Is that Grandma a-coming?" Myrl asks, in her pretend world once more.

"I reckon it is," answers Deacon Girl in a tender voice. "She looks happy, doesn't she?"

"Yes, she does ..."

That afternoon all is quiet until I get a visitor of my own. He comes in with one of the aides and stands by my bed.

"How is Mother today?" he asks.

"No change," says the aide. "Doesn't respond at all."

BIG BOB

Carol Manley
Springfield, IL

I did not have sex with Big Bob Miller for a chili recipe. I know people think I did, but if all you had to do for a good recipe was to sleep with somebody, I know a whole lot of women who'd be much better cooks than what they are.

I'm a Christian woman. You won't find me seeking financial gain through anything I do. It's all out of Christian charity.

There's plenty of women who'll give that Christian charity to a man who's young and good looking. But I think it's a lot more Christian to give it to a man who smells like onions and looks lonely all the time.

Big Bob was a sweet old guy. If you went in the shop just once, he'd remember you forever. And when you left and he said "come back soon" he had a kind of yearning in his voice like he really meant it. I can't believe nobody else noticed how lonely he was. He had pictures on the wall of himself with all the past mayors and county fair queens with their arms trying to reach around him while he held the chili cook-off trophy every year for the past three decades. But he didn't seem to have any friends.

That's how folks are and that's the lesson I'm taking with me: you gotta watch out for folks who love your chili recipe more than they love you.

I really got to know Bob one day when I went in the restaurant with a dollar and forty seven cents. He asked me what would I like and I asked him what I could get for a dollar and forty-seven cents. He plunked down the biggest bowl of chili you ever saw. "Keep your money," he said. "Just tell me what you think of my secret ingredient."

Bob was always talking about secret ingredients like he was changing the recipe every day, but that chili tasted exactly the same every day of Bob's life if you ate it at the restaurant. He tried a lot of secret ingredients at home, but none of them ever got past the privacy of his kitchen.

But that day I didn't know what to say to him. "Bob, your secret ingredient's too secret for me," I said and left it at that. Then I asked if he needed some help with the dishes. He got the biggest smile you ever saw on his face and he had just the big, round face for it. Course it coulda been just his high blood pressure blushing up his face, but I think he was happy to have my help.

I dried a few dishes for him and that's when folks started thinking I was after the man's chili recipe. I say it's a darned shame that folks don't know the difference between gold-digging and Christian charity.

They really got talking when we starting going to garage sales together.

You woulda thought we were slipping off to a motel somewhere the way people looked at us when climbed into Bob's big old LeSabre with the Saturday morning paper folded open to the classifieds.

Bob liked to find big old pots and soup ladles. I bought jigsaw puzzles and Frank Sinatra records. One thing about Frank Sinatra, you can think you got every record he ever made and then you go to a garage sale and find one you never saw before. Big Bob and Frank Sinatra had that in common, they could be surprising and predictable at the same time. I'd always pray a little over the jigsaw puzzles if they'd already been opened because I needed God to direct me as to whether all the pieces were there or not. But I never had to ask God whether or not to buy the record albums. God loves Frank Sinatra.

Garage sales are only good until about noon. By then folks have scooped up the good stuff and all they have left is household decorations made out of dried twigs and maternity clothes with ketchup stains on them. So we'd usually get back to Big Bob's house right around lunch time.

We'd go straight to the kitchen. I'd put on some Sinatra and work the puzzles on his kitchen table while he experimented with secret ingredients to put in chili. He had an old record player in the kitchen on top of a big old console TV next to the recliner, which I think made for a very well furnished kitchen.

Then one Saturday, while Bob was cooking and I was working a new jigsaw puzzle, Little Bob came walking in the door like he owned the place. It was shock to me because I didn't know there was a Little Bob. But there was. And he was standing there casting a shadow over my jigsaw puzzle. Frank Sinatra started to stutter and Big Bob lifted the needle off the record. Little Bob was bigger than Big Bob. And didn't have any of his personality.

Turned out, when I got the story later, Big Bob had been married to a woman who had run off with a mailman. I thought that was against the code of the postal service, but you never know what some people will do. It had been thirty years or more. Shirley had taken Little Bob and her mailman and run off to some unknown postal code causing Big Bob to not trust anybody anymore. A while after that, Shirley left that mailman for an encyclopedia salesman who she left for a man who sold aluminum siding before she finally took up with some kind of preacher which I think suggests that she was a fickle hearted woman, but Big Bob blamed himself. He was that kind of guy.

Little Bob was big and round like his daddy, but there was something cold and hard at core of him. He eyed me like we were standing in a boxing ring, though he faked like he was friendly. He picked up a puzzle piece like he knew where it went. But he didn't. I had only just started putting together the edge pieces and he was fumbling around with a piece that looked like a tongue. The picture was a basket of puppies with their tongues hanging out. I looked at the cover of the box. The puppies looked like they didn't trust Little Bob, either.

"Daddy, we need a family discussion," he said, looking at me hard. "Just family." Like he thought I was going to crawl into a hole somewhere. Well, I did slip out the room, but since Frank Sinatra had gotten silenced for stuttering,

I could hear the discussion anyway.

Turned out Little Bob lived about five hundred miles away, but somebody had called to tell him that his Daddy's chili recipe was in danger. Since neither the mailman nor the encyclopedia salesman nor the man who sold aluminum siding had left his mother anything but unsatisfied, that chili recipe seemed like it was going to be the only heritage Little Bob was likely to get in this world. The preacher that his mom had ended up with was planning on taking all his treasure to heaven with him. Sounded like the man was half-way Christian and half-way King Tut.

Little Bob had his heart set on that recipe. Some folks don't ever think about trying to get what they want by being nice. They just managed by meanness. Little Bob set about making his dad feel bad. He reminded Big Bob that, in spite of the mailman and the encyclopedia salesman and the man who sold aluminum siding and the preacher, Big Bob was still legally married to Little Bob's mother. "The whole town's talking about you," he told Big Bob.

Well, I knew it wasn't the whole town. It was just Thelma Sue whose husband used to deliver Big Bob's mail. Thelma Sue would have been willing to accept the trade when Big Bob's wife ran off with her husband, but Big Bob never understood subtlety. He had reminded her she was a married woman and she never spoke to him again. That's what he told me anyway. When her mailman husband never came back and Big Bob never accepted her consolation, Thelma Sue remained bitter. And Big Bob remained lonely until that day I dried his dishes.

Big Bob was looking very embarrassed when Little Bob left and he had to explain to me why the garage sales and secret ingredients had to stop.

"I ain't worried about myself," he said, "but I don't want folks talking about you like you was some kind of floozy." That kinda broke my heart. I figure that if you really are a Christian woman, then it don't matter what anybody thinks about you. That's all between you and God. But Big Bob didn't want to spoil my earthly reputation with any more garage sales. We divided up the Sinatra records and I left him looking mournful in his kitchen recliner.

Next time I went into the restaurant, Big Bob looked sad. I wanted to console him, but I knew he needed some convincing. I looked around and gave a big sigh. "How many folks you figure going to get saved in here?" Big Bob looked confused.

"Well," I got more specific, "if anything happens to you, the restaurant's going to end up with your wife and that preacher. I figure they know more about saving souls than cooking chili. But they'll appreciate having a cash register."

Big Bob filed for his divorce the next day. Soon as it was final, we were back on the garage sale circuit. I had reunited the Sinatra records in Bob's kitchen and starting collecting Tony Bennett. I sprayed some air freshener on that recliner where the fried onion smell had gotten a whole lot stronger. Then I went back to giving Big Bob all the Christian charity I had to give. We turned back the arm on the record player so it kept playing the same side over and over one night and it must have been about the fifteenth time that Tony Bennett left his heart in San Francisco when Big Bob's heart stopped.

I jumped up and called the paramedics. It was too late. "Don't blame yourself, Lady," the older one said to me as we were waiting for the coroner. Everybody knew Big Bob was the Chili King. His arteries had to be so clogged that Liquid Plumber couldn't have cleaned them out.

I changed Tony Bennett to Frank Sinatra and watched them wheel Big Bob out. Then I put away all his chili ingredients that he always kept lined up on the counter, thankful that he hadn't died alone.

Soon as they knew he was dead, everybody in town tried to act like they were his best friend. Not one of them had ever offered to dry his dishes.

Folks who had lost all hope of ever winning a chili cook-off perked up and polished up their spatulas. They all wanted the Chili King crown and nobody wanted to wait for the county fair. It was decided that the best way to honor Big Bob would be with a combination funeral and chili cook-off. That way he could go to his eternal rest knowing that there was a new Chili King. Nature abhors a vacuum.

When the day came, Little Bob brought his mother who had the nerve to wear a black veil and she brought her preacher paramour who gave the eulogy. He had never met Big Bob, but made up for it with a whole sermon of chili metaphors.

We endured about an hour of that preacher talking about how Big Bob "seasoned all our lives" while people squirmed around in their seats wanting to get back to stirring their pots.

As soon as that lame sermon was over, we all headed to the church basement where our chili was simmering away. Even though it was a House of God, most people had put locks on their pots. The competition was that intense. With Big Bob out of the way, it was a wide-open field. They all eyed me suspiciously. I thought it was very sad that none of those people had any correct understanding of Christian charity. They might be in the habit of getting recipes by devious means, but I am not.

The judge moved around the room like Goldilocks. He pronounced one pot too spicy and one too bland, one too sweet and one too sour. Alpha Ortega had put fishheads in his and the judge passed him by completely, not knowing that Big Bob had once experimented with a Lenten chili made with sardines. Anna Loraine offered him a jar of her homemade pickles but he refused the bribery and moved on. He disqualified Sunshine Baldwin's vegetarian chili for not having any meat. Then he arrived at mine.

I had not locked up my pot while we were off tending to Big Bob. I just left God in charge of it, knowing that God loves chili just as much as he loves Frank Sinatra. If anybody had sabotaged my recipe, they'd have to answer to the Creator of all mankind. And none of them wanted to do that. The judge approached.

Silence fell over the room as everyone sucked in their breath at once. They'd all been sweet and friendly to my face, but I knew what they were saying about me and my Christian charity and what I had done to get that recipe. And they knew I knew it. They avoided my eyes.

I lifted the lid off my pot. The judge dipped in his spoon and raised it to his lips. People were getting faint from holding their breath. I watched the judge's eyes flutter and roll back in his head. He teetered a moment before regaining his balance. "Ah," he said. "That's chili!" He placed the blue ribbon on my pot.

I saw folks exchange knowing glances. I looked at the judge and then raised my eyes toward the ceiling to where I was sure Big Bob rested much easier. I thanked the judge and then silently told Big Bob that it was okay for him go on to the mansion that was prepared for him in eternity. "My Father's house has many mansions," Jesus had said. And I knew that one of them had a big old recliner in the kitchen.

Little Bob inherited the restaurant, but he couldn't run it and ended up selling it to somebody who made it into a sushi bar. When he had a garage sale of Big Bob's things, I bought the recliner. It's a comfort to me, though I still haven't gotten the fried onion smell out of it. I retired that blue ribbon.

Haven't even eaten any chili since that funeral. I saw what it did to Bob and figured I'd better watch my cholesterol. I want to live a long life to enjoy the money I made from selling that recipe to the company that has all those commercials on TV.

Folks continue to talk about me behind my back, but it doesn't worry me. I gave the man nothing but good Christian charity. And if the man cooked me chili in return, the least I could do was pay attention while he cooked it.

AZIZ

Jasmin Darznick
Tiburon, CA

When she named her last child, my great-grandmother indulged her fantasies at last, conjuring deserts and *djinn* and powers beyond imagining. "Kobra," she announced to the midwife and smiled from the bloodstained sheets. "The snake."

Chosen under the watchful gaze of her own mother and mother-in-law, the names of her other eight children made up an unremarkable roster of Muslim names—Hassan, Fatemeh, Mahmoud, and so on. But by the time of her last child's birth both her mother and mother-in-law were dead and she herself was called old, and so the list of her children's names settled finally on one of her own choice, "Kobra."

Thereafter, it was commonly suspected that my great-grandmother had lost her mind, and possibly also her faith.

Everyone feared for the child.

But Kobra grew up to be the prettiest girl of the family, with the only pair of honey-colored eyes in the house. And with her beauty came a temper so gentle that it dispelled every suspicion about her mother's piety and her own virtue.

In Iran they call such children the pearls of their mothers' fortunes.

Around her neck Kobra wore a black string from which a single, tiny blue eye hung and nestled itself in the hollow of her throat. The amulet was meant to protect her from the Evil Eye, which had bedeviled her mother since the day of Kobra's birth—so fearful was she that jealous eyes would alight on her favorite child.

When Kobra was ten years old, her mother decided that as the last of so many children, it was unlikely she would ever marry. For this reason, she explained, it would be necessary to send her to a school that prepared young girls to become professional seamstresses.

Many secretly believed that my great-grandmother wished to keep this one child for herself, and it was for this reason that of all her daughters it was Kobra whom she sent from the house to learn a trade. But whatever the reason, from then on Kobra could be seen each morning stepping into the streets of Tehran, kerchief knotted at her chin, with a basket of fabric and needles in one hand and a small, iron pot filled with rice and stew in the other.

***

Then one night her brother Hassan, the gambler, settled a debt that altered my grandmother's fortune forever. Late one evening, after losing a great sum of money—his greatest loss yet in what would be a long and infamous career—Hassan turned to his gambling partner and said, "You can take my sister." He did not name her at all, but added simply, "The youngest one."

Hassan returned home that same night with news that he'd found Kobra a suitor, and the news was met there with unbridled glee. Her sisters tittered and giggled, her aunts clucked their tongues and smiled. Shoja was so handsome and came from so highly regarded a family that even my great-grandmother took Hassan's news as a stroke of incredibly good luck.

And so, with their mother's consent, Hassan's debts were neatly covered by what would have been Kobra's dowry and my fourteen-year old grandmother became, for a time, Arooseh Khanoomeh Djafari.

In Iran young brides have no name. Known simply as "aroos," or the "bride," they only really take their husbands' names when their mother-in-laws die. When my grandmother was called "aroos" her hair fell in black braids, thick as coiled ropes, down to the middle of her back. She was shy, neat, and modest, which Shoja knew would endear her to his mother, the widowed Khanoom Jafari. But however beautiful Kobra's eyes and plaits of black hair, she was simple, provincial, and as unlikely a match for my grandfather's elegance and airs as, it would seem, she was for her own fantastical name.

My grandfather came from a clan whose women were, if anything, even more devout than the women in my grandmother's family. The Djafaris were one of the several hundred families in Iran who claimed direct descent from the Prophet Mohammad and Shoja himself held the title of *sey-yed*, which designates a kind of Shiite royalty in Iran. Yet my grandfather's own disposition and tastes aligned him with the part of Iran whose ambitions were thoroughly modern and Western. He dressed in perfectly tailored Western suits, then still rare in Iran, and drove a Black Chrysler of which they say he was no less vain than of his own brilliantined hair.

For several years Shoja had courted the favor of a lady so chic it was said she could pass for a foreigner's wife. But this woman was older and unable to bear children; Shoja knew that until he produced heirs to his family name, he could never marry her.

As a sey-yed, Shoja held several important privileges of his faith, one of which was that he could divorce his wife by uttering a single line of Islamic law. So after Kobra bore him a daughter and then two sons, Shoja invoked this privilege to undo her claims to his family name and enter a long-desired marriage to his mistress. At that moment Kobra became Khanoom Hassan—the name of her own recently dead mother.

The name change was a disaster attended by a gesture nearly as damning: the swift slamming of her husband's hand on her face when he sent her from the house. As she had no money for a proper surgery, the neighborhood doctor would do no more than slice the crushed bones from her face and bind her nose with gauze to quell the blood. By the next morning she would awaken to find the flesh of her nose had collapsed and spread across the middle of her face, and you might have said (as many did) that from then on her honey-colored eyes were wasted on her.

"Who can understand the ways of God?" her aunt had remarked. "It was *gesmat.*"

None of her children called her mother, or "Maman," again. Because in Iran children have traditionally been the property of fathers, after my grandmother left, my mother, who was then seven, stayed on with her younger brothers to be raised by her paternal grandmother and aunts. For several years my grandmother did not see her children, except on the afternoons when she stood outside the gates of their school, waiting to catch sight of them. She'd call out their names, slip a handkerchief filled with honeyed candies through the bars of the gate, and warn them not to forget her.

***

In 1936, as part of a massive modernization campaign, the Emperor Reza Shah outlawed the veil in Iran. From then on a woman caught in a chador on the streets of any village, town, or city in Iran would have the chador torn from her body. If she resisted she would be beaten, jailed, fined.

After my grandfather divorced her, my grandmother had supported herself by sewing chadors and modest housedresses for women of the neighborhood. But with the imperial edict forbidding the veil, she found herself with a huge clientele of women in sudden, desperate need of the slacks, dresses, and two-piece suits with which Iranian women were to make their way into the future.

My grandmother profited handsomely under the Emperor's new law.

Then, not long after this, the news came that my grandfather had died, struck dead by the car of a Western diplomat as he was crossing a street in Tehran. My grandmother was forbidden from attending his funeral; it was his second wife who bore that particular honor. But when this lady herself died just a few years later, it was my grandmother who stood, hair bobbed now and in round-toed heels, to give her name as Khanoom Djafari to an unwitting government clerk and thereby claim the plot of earth next to Shoja's in a graveyard outside Tehran.

I have never heard my grandmother speak of my grandfather, but I do know that she has always been exceedingly proud of this plot of earth and that she is known—still—to hire a taxi to drive and visit it from time to time.

***

Toward the middle of her life my grandmother opened a beauty shop in Tehran, which she called "Lady Diola." The name was a fantasy and a fiction—invented by her to sound both French and modern. It was also a gamble she won, because for two decades the ladies of Tehran passed through her doors calling out, "Salam, Diola khanoom!" My grandmother did not correct them,

38

just smiled silently over her pots of henna, tucking away the bills that would later amount to a fortune envied by every one of her siblings still left living.

In the afternoons when I was a child, my mother used to leave me at my grandmother's salon while she ran errands in the city. After she finished her work, my grandmother would take me to her bedroom in her small apartment behind the salon. There she sewed me dolls with velvet tunics, satin slippers, and real golden hoops pierced through their tiny cotton ears. She lined both my wrists with rows of bangles and strung a blue-eyed amulet around my neck just as, she told me, her mother had done for her. Then we would lie down side by side on her narrow bed and she would tell me tales about a rapacious deev and the princess who bewitched him with a dance.

And while I slept on some of those afternoons in Tehran, my grandmother would steal away to the bathroom and with eyeliner and lipstick draw on her stomach a set of enormous eyes, thick, vermillion lips, and a black beauty mark as round and as fat as a coin. She'd sit on the edge of the bed, waiting for me to awake, and then she would begin to dance.

My grandmother strained and stretched her belly, let it loose and drew it in, arranged and rearranged the painted features so that her stomach turned into a live, wriggling kaleidoscope of expressions.

I didn't know this yet, but it was a dance that Iranian women had performed for each other in the *andaroon*, or women's quarters, for hundreds of years. It was a vestige of the all-but vanished country to which she had been born, the place she conjured for me in the stories and songs that still make up my own best memories of Iran.

But what haunts me still is neither the dance itself nor the face of the woman she drew, but the canvas of my grandmother's flesh. Dimpled and slack in the middle, the peripheries of her stomach were streaked with what looked to me like claw marks. My own belly was round but perfectly taut as a honeydew; I had no idea yet how a woman's body could change, the common, timeless violence that brings these transformations.

There was so much that I saw and didn't understand.

So maybe it is not the memory of her body, but the memory of my own innocence that haunts me. Because I am imagining myself in those moments, looking at my grandmother without the words to make up a story. I am thinking of all stories I have heard and all the stories I have needed to make up—and thinking, too, that my memories will always elude the grasp of my words.

But in the time before I knew anything, really, about my grandmother's life, before I learned to hold each story I heard about her up to the unnatural light of my own imagining, my grandmother's belly was magical to me. I could hold her in my eyes then. And after she danced, when she gathered me in her arms and I pressed my palm into her face, loving the yielding softness of her nose, she did not push away my hand.

I knew her by one name, Aziz, which means "dear one" in Farsi.

ABIQUIU

Judith Hemenway
Del Mar, CA

The land here is all skin and bones,
A hide stretched from horizon to horizon:
Wrinkled, pocked, parched,
Its mesas and mountains jutting through
The surface at odd angles,
Bleeding red clay.

Brown mud courses through its veins,
Draining what little moisture there is,
Carrying it down into the dark places,
Cutting deep through layers of time.
Crackled canyons echo jagged lightning
And hurl its thunder back into
The massing clouds.

Witches howl through the hills,
A steer skull marks the path,
Blank white and unblinking,
Flowers float on waves of heat,
And a pale, pale ghost in the night blue sky
Blesses the Pedernal
With its magical light.

Here one can rise and open,
And drink the sky forever,
And be nourished beyond comprehension.
Even the grasses swallow the sun,
Glowing green tufts spurting
Exuberantly from the dead skin
Of this dry land.

I long to climb the ladder as she did,
And sit serenely on the roof,
Wrapt in the soft cool darkness,
Sipping the stars.

MOM'S CANOE

Rebecca Foust
Ross, CA

Do you remember your old canoe?
Wooden wide-bellied, tapered ends
made to slip through tight riverbends
swiftly, like shadow.

Hull ribbed delicately, wing of bird;
sometimes seen, never heard
when it flew through the water,
more glider than boat,
ponderous in portage, weightless afloat.
Wide, shallow saucer, vessel of air
frail origami, suspended where
shallows met shadows.

Remember how the wood glowed like honey in summer
as you rubbed it with beeswax and turpentine
against leaks and cracks, weather and time.
All the housekeeping you had in you
Went into caring for that canoe,
and it rode high, bow lifted,
arced up, like flight—
all magic and power and evening light.
You j-stroking, side-slipping, eddying out
frugal with movement, all without
effort, just like you walked and ran,
breathed, sang, loved, and swam.

I still see you rising from water to sky,
paddle held high,
river drops limning its edge.
Brown diamonds catch the light as you lift, then dip.
Parting the current, you slip
silently through the evening shadows.

You, birdsong, watersong, slanting light,
following riverbend, swallowed from sight

41

SMALL THINGS

Cary Pepper
San Francisco, CA

CHARACTERS: HOYT   50s. Tall. Deliberate. Tired.
DREW   19. Clean-cut, well-scrubbed. Innocent,
sincere. Gives the impression of being almost fragile.

HOYT'S apartment.

(Stage Right, a couch, in front of which is a coffee table. Stage Left, an easy chair.)

HOYT sits on the couch, cleaning a revolver. The doorbell rings. HOYT glances at the door, but doesn't move. The bell rings again. HOYT thinks ... then tucks the pistol under a couch cushion, goes to the door, and opens it. In the doorway is DREW, who has started to walk away. When HOYT opens the door, he stops. DREW is clean-cut and well scrubbed. He wears a suit and tie, neither of which look natural on him. He carries a briefcase, which also seems out of place: it should be carried by an accountant or a businessman twice his age.)

DREW
Oh. I didn't think anyone was home.

HOYT
No one is.

DREW
Uh, I represent the Assembly of Hubristic Evangelicals. We ...

HOYT
The what?

DREW
The Assembly of Hubristic Evangelicals. Have you experienced the one true god?

HOYT

Not lately.

DREW

Well, if you'll give me just a few minutes, I'll tell you how you can experience the one true god.

HOYT

Right now?

DREW

There's no more perfect time to experience the one true god than the moment he comes to you.

HOYT

Has he come to me?

DREW

He will, if you open yourself to his love and his power.

HOYT

Right now?

DREW

There's no more perfect time to experience the one true god than the moment he comes to you. May I counsel with you?

HOYT

Now?

DREW

There's no more perfect time to ...

HOYT

Experience the one true god. Got it. To tell you the truth ...

DREW

There is only one truth. That of the one true god.

(HOYT gazes at DREW.)

DREW

That truth will save you.

(HOYT's gaze becomes a stare.)

And when ... you ... experience ...

(Something in HOYT's stare causes to DREW to hesitate ...)

this ... experience ...

(then falter...)

it ... strikes ... you ... dumb ...

(then stop.)

... with awe.

(HOYT continues to stare ... DREW stands there ...
dumbstruck with awe ... LONG PAUSE.)

HOYT

Oh, this ... is ... perfect.

DREW

Well ... Sorry to have ...

(He turns to go.)

HOYT

Come in.

DREW

What?

HOYT

Come in.

DREW

Really?

HOYT

Yes. I want to be struck dumb with awe.

(HOYT steps back. DREW enters uncertainly.)

DREW

Thank you. For allowing me to ....

                    HOYT
Sit down.

          (DREW starts for the couch.)

                    HOYT
Not there.

                    DREW
Sorry.

          (HOYT motions toward the chair.)

                    HOYT
Here. Sit there.

          (DREW sits in the chair. HOYT sits on the couch. His hand
     automatically goes to the cushion, on top of where he put the pistol.
          DREW seems to be thrown, uncertain of himself.)

                    (PAUSE.)

                    HOYT
So ... Strike me.

                    DREW
Excuse me?

                    HOYT
Strike me dumb with awe.

                    DREW
Oh ... There is only one true god.

                    HOYT
Is there?

                    DREW
Yes. And he ...

                    HOYT
And you know who he is.

                    DREW
Yes. He's the ...

HOYT

When you say you know who he is ... You mean you, personally? Or the entire Assembly of Hubristic Evangelicals?

DREW

Oh, yes. All of us. For we have ...

HOYT

How old are you?

DREW

Nineteen. Well, I'll be nineteen in two days.

HOYT

Aren't you a little young for this?

DREW

We all do it. Everyone in the assembly does a year of missionary work when they turn eighteen.

HOYT

You're nineteen.

DREW

Yes.

HOYT

So ... you're ... extra evangelical?

DREW

I'm finishing my year of missionary service. Today's my last day.

HOYT

And how does that make you feel?

DREW

Relieved! Uh ... To experience the one true god ...

HOYT

What's his name?

DREW

Who?

HOYT

The one true god.

DREW

His names are many. His spirit is omnipresent ... His power is omnipotent ... His love is ...

HOYT

But what do you call him?

DREW

Who?

HOYT

The one true god.

DREW

... God.

HOYT

That's it? God?

DREW

Those who know the one true god need no other name. His spirit and power dwell within us. His essence flows through us like an endless stream of eternal sustenance. His glory ...

HOYT

But he has no name.

DREW

Who?

HOYT

God.

DREW

Once you experience the one true god, he is within you, and you within him. Only the uninitiated need an earthly name for him. For they have not felt his power and glory.

HOYT

And you want to ... initiate me?

DREW

Only the Initiated can experience the one true god.

HOYT

So, the rest of us can't?

DREW

Until you're Initiated, you have no true concept of god.

HOYT

What about my religion?

DREW

There is only one true faith.

HOYT

Yours.

DREW

Only the Initiated know the true path. Only the Initiated see the true light.

HOYT

So the rest of us are just stumbling around in darkness.

DREW

Only the Initiated experience the true sublimity of knowing the one true god.

HOYT

OK. How do we do this?

DREW

What?

HOYT

How do I get to see the true light?

DREW

You become Initiated.

HOYT

Right. How do I do that?

DREW

What?

HOYT

Get initiated.

DREW

You join the Assembly of Hubristic Evangelicals.

HOYT

How do I do that?

DREW

What?

HOYT

Join the club. Become a hubristic evangelical. I want to see the true light. I want to experience the one true god.

DREW

Oh ... I have some pamphlets here ... These explain, pretty much ...

(DREW takes pamphlets out of his briefcase and puts them on the table. HOYT picks up the pamphlets and reads their titles.)

HOYT

"The One True Path to the One True God" ... "The One True God and You" ... "Being Hubristic" ... "Be God and Be Good" ...

DREW
(Handing over another pamphlet)

And this pamphlet will tell you about our bible. ... The One True Book. We combined the old and new testaments, took out the parts that are wrong, and revealed the one true message of the one true god. You'll get your own bible when you're Initiated.

HOYT

Yeah, let's do that.

DREW

What?

HOYT

Get initiated.

DREW

Well, if you come to a meeting, you can speak to a ...

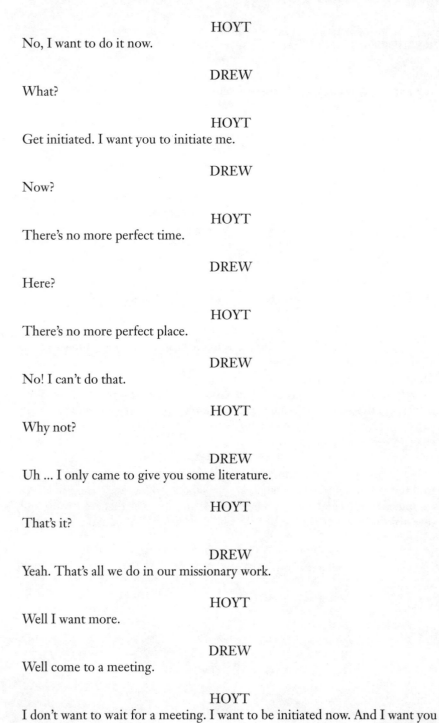

HOYT

No, I want to do it now.

DREW

What?

HOYT

Get initiated. I want you to initiate me.

DREW

Now?

HOYT

There's no more perfect time.

DREW

Here?

HOYT

There's no more perfect place.

DREW

No! I can't do that.

HOYT

Why not?

DREW

Uh ... I only came to give you some literature.

HOYT

That's it?

DREW

Yeah. That's all we do in our missionary work.

HOYT

Well I want more.

DREW

Well come to a meeting.

HOYT

I don't want to wait for a meeting. I want to be initiated now. And I want you to do it.

                    DREW

I've never done that!

                    HOYT

No one's ever asked you to?

                    DREW

No one's ever let me in!

                    HOYT

You've been doing this for a year and no one's let you in?

                    DREW

No!

                    HOYT

That must be frustrating.

                    DREW

It totally sucks!

                    HOYT

Well, you've hit the jackpot this time. You're going all the way, son. Initiate me.

                    DREW

Uh ... Why don't you read the pamphlets. And then you can ...

                    HOYT

I'll read the pamphlets later. Just go ahead and do ... whatever needs to be done.

                    DREW

I can't.

                    HOYT

Why not?

                    DREW

Um ... uh ... I'm not an elder.

                    HOYT

But you've been initiated, right?

                         DREW
Yeah. When I was, like, seven.

                         HOYT
OK. Do to me, what they did to you.

                         DREW
I can't!

                         HOYT
Why not? What'd they do to you?

                         DREW
They ... had me stand before the Assembly ... and ... they ... Gestured over me
... and they ... Questioned me ... and I answered rightly ... and they ... Gestured
over me some more.

                         HOYT
That's it?

                         DREW
That was it.

                         HOYT
Did you feel initiated?

                         DREW
Yeah.

                         HOYT
Did you feel different?

                         DREW
Yeah! I was Initiated!

                         HOYT
Did you know the one true path?

                         DREW
I was Initiated!

                         HOYT
Did you know the one true god?

DREW

We all did! We were all Initiated!

HOYT

Did you see the true light?

DREW

Well ... no. They said that would come later. All the older people said they saw it.

HOYT

What did you feel?

DREW

When?

HOYT

When you were initiated.

DREW

Feel? I'd been initiated!

HOYT

Did you feel happy?

DREW

Yeah!

HOYT

Did you feel special?

DREW

YEAH!

HOYT

Did you feel at peace?

DREW

I was seven.

HOYT

Right. OK ... So. Just do to me what they did to you.

DREW

I can't.

HOYT

Why not?

DREW

I shouldn't.

HOYT

Why not?

DREW

It wouldn't be right.

HOYT

Why not?

DREW

I'd rather not say.

HOYT

I won't tell anyone.

DREW

No. I'd rather not.

HOYT

C'mon. It's just you and me. And I'm about to become one of you. You've done your job well. You've got a convert. Your first one. They'll love you for this.

DREW

They'll hate me.

HOYT

No they won't.

DREW

They already hate me.

HOYT

Would that be the one true hate?

DREW

Might as well be.

HOYT

Do they believe in hate?

54

DREW

Not officially.

HOYT

Well, they sound like everyone else on that one. So ... Convert me! Initiate me!

DREW

It wouldn't be right.

HOYT
(He will not be denied)

Why?

DREW

Because I'm leaving the Assembly.

HOYT

Something you haven't mentioned?

DREW

Could I ... have a glass of water? Or something?

HOYT

Sure. Would you prefer water? Or something?

DREW

No ... water will be fine, thanks.

(HOYT goes into the kitchen. DREW sits looking at the floor, deflated. HOYT returns with a glass of water and gives it to DREW.)

DREW

Thanks.
(He gulps down all the water.)

HOYT

We're a little thirsty.

DREW

I guess.

HOYT

Want some more?

                    DREW

No, thanks.

                    HOYT

So ... Why are you leaving?

                    DREW

I'd rather not say.

                    HOYT

It's a little late for that.

                    DREW

What do you mean?

                    HOYT

You started this.

                    DREW

What?

                    HOYT

The forced intimacy.

                    DREW

I don't know what you're ...

                    HOYT

You ring my bell ... you interrupt what I'm doing ... you come into my house
... and you immediately question my religious beliefs. Then you challenge my
beliefs ... invalidate them ... And try to impose your beliefs on me.

                    DREW

I ... I never thought of it that way.

                    HOYT

What did you think you were doing?

                    DREW

Spreading the one true word.

                    HOYT

Why do you want to do that?

                    DREW

They tell us to.

                    HOYT

So you just go out and do it?

                    DREW

We all do.

                    HOYT

What makes you think I want to hear about your religion?

                    DREW

It's the one true faith.

                    HOYT

For you. Maybe I've got my own faith.

                    DREW

Ours is the one true religion.

                    HOYT

How do you know mine isn't the one true religion?

                    DREW

There can be only one true religion.

                    HOYT

Well maybe it's mine!

                    DREW

It can't be.

                    HOYT

Why not?

                    DREW

Because it's mine.

                    HOYT

How do you know that?

                    DREW

The one true book tells us it is.

                    HOYT
Who wrote this book?

                    DREW
The one true prophet.

                    HOYT
This is one hot belief system, huh?

                    DREW
It's the one true religion.

                    HOYT
So why are you quitting?

                    DREW
I'd rather not say.

                    [MORE]

WAIT IT OUT

Clint Till
Birmingham, AL

INT. MOUNTAIN CABIN—AFTERNOON (DAY ONE)

A sparse cabin, during a heavy winter storm.

The door opens. Two MEN enter, carrying a BODY in a tarp. The larger, GRIZZLY MAN enters first. Carrying the legs of the corpse is an intelligent looking accomplice, wearing round-rimmed eyeglasses. We'll call him GLASSES. They carry the body to the back door, where they drop it with a loud THUD. A younger, NERVOUS MAN rushes in.

> NERVOUS MAN
> What were you thinking? You know what they're going to do to us if we're caught? I'm no murderer. I don't need this added to my sentence!

The Grizzly Man rushes up to the Nervous Man.

> GRIZZLY MAN
> You wanna shut up for just one minute?!

Two more men enter—one is tall, slender, dark hair—soft features. He carries a NOTEBOOK by his side. We'll call him NOTEBOOK. The other is shorter, but his face looks rougher—more chiseled. We'll call him CHISELED MAN.

> CHISELED MAN
> Settle down Dell.

> GRIZZLY MAN
> (referring to the Nervous Man) This pussy is gonna blow the whole arrangement! We'll never make it with him here!

> NOTEBOOK
> He'll be fine. He's my responsibility.

NERVOUS MAN

I don't need you to baby-sit me, Frank!

CHISELED MAN

Every one calm down. Our situation now is a lot better than it was four days ago. We're out, and we're only a couple of days from the border.

GRIZZLY MAN

At the most. We didn't need to stop here.

GLASSES

I have to agree with Dell on this one, Roe. At this point we need to put distance between ourselves and the state troopers.

Notebook (Frank) busies himself with studying their surroundings. He drifts into the BEDROOM unnoticed by the others.

Frank peers over his shoulder to make sure that he isn't being watched. He then turns, opens his large overcoat and removes A SMALL BRIEFCASE.

He makes his way to one side of the bed, kneels down and runs his fingers along the hardwood floors.

Frank pries up a loose floorboard, revealing a small space underneath. He lowers the case into the hole and replaces the board.

CHISELED MAN (ROE) (O.S.)

They won't pick up our route for a few more hours. We have time.

NERVOUS MAN (O.S.)

(referring to the corpse) Killing this guy didn't help the situation!

GRIZZLY MAN (DELL) (O.S.)

Would you shut up! I had to do it!

NERVOUS MAN (O.S.)

No one said for you to kill him!

ROE (O.S.)

We can't do anything about it now.

GLASSES (O.S.)

Give it a rest Tony.

DELL (O.S.)
I don't need anybody to tell me what to do!

NERVOUS MAN (TONY) (O.S.)
We'll all be picked up in a matter of hours, thanks to that stunt!

ROE (O.S.)
Shut up! All of you!

Frank returns to the LIVING ROOM just as Dell and Tony charge each other. Tony lands a solid punch to Dell's jaw, but the effect is minimal.

Dell counters with a jab to the stomach. Tony doubles over, unable to catch his breath.

Tony charges again, wrapping himself around Dell's waist. They fall to the floor.

Frank rushes in to pull Tony from the fray. Yuri grabs Dell.

Dell tries to charge again, but Glasses blocks him.

DELL
You do that again and I'll kill you!

TONY
You shouldn't even be here!

ROE
Stop!

Tony breathes heavily. His nose is bloody.

Glasses pushes Dell back to the table. Frank pulls Tony toward the front door.

FRANK
Go to the car and get the sacks.

TONY
What?

FRANK
The food. It's in the car. Could you please get it?

                          DELL
          Yeah, kid. I'm starving. Make yourself useful.

Tony walks toward the door.

                          ROE
          And pull the truck around to the back.

                          TONY
          (under his breath) I don't believe this.

                          ROE
What?

                          TONY
Nothing.

Tony exits, Frank crosses to the window, looking around at the surrounding
cabins. Roe approaches him and glances up at the sky.

                          ROE
          Everyone's on edge. And this weather isn't helping.

                          FRANK
          I know, but we needed the rest.

                          ROE
          We should start out a little earlier, but I don't want to take the chance
          of someone recognizing that SUV.

Frank reaches for his notebook. He flips through the pages, each one filled with
neat, handwritten notes. He stops, scans the page, and checks his watch.

                          FRANK
          We still have a few hours.

Frank reads more then places the book back into his pocket.

                          DELL
          (calling to Frank) Jeez, man. How long does it take for your kid
          brother to get a few sacks out of the car?

                          FRANK
Don't worry about it Dell.

Glasses walks up to Roe.

GLASSES

We need to take care of our little package back there.

ROE

You and Dell can dump him after we eat.

Tony re-enters with the sacks of food. Dell scrambles to his feet and starts searching through the bags.

TONY

Slow down, man.

DELL

Hey, screw you! Killing a man always makes me hungry. Where are my onion rings?

TONY

You're sick.

DELL

Yeah, probably, but it feels so good.

Dell grabs a hamburger and onion rings. He sits at the table. Tony places the other sacks on the coffee table. They all take their food.

GLASSES

(to Dell) Roe wants us to dump the body after we eat.

DELL

Fine, but I'm taking his watch before we get rid of him.

ROE

No souvenirs, Dell.

DELL

What?

ROE

It's bad enough that you stabbed him, but we don't need anything linking us with his death.

DELL

Come on, Roe. You gotta admit, when his eyes got wide and he started gasping for air, that was golden.

TONY
Hey, I'm eating over here.

DELL
You shut your mouth! I was talking to Roe! Frank, tell your brother to keep quiet before I slice him like the old man in there!

TONY
He's not my boss!

FRANK
Just eat! Rest up. We still have a long way to drive tonight.

Peace is restored and the small group continues their meal.

GLASSES
(to Dell) Why did you have to kill him?

DELL
Aw, come on, Yuri. You saw the way he was looking at that truck, and at us. He wanted to be a hero. I had to do it. Plus, I enjoyed it.

GLASSES (YURI)
How could you possibly enjoy it?

DELL
Don't knock it 'til you try it.

YURI
No thanks. I'm not like you.

DELL
Most people aren't. It takes a certain quality to be like me.

YURI
A psychotic mind, hell-bent on destruction just for the pleasure of it?

DELL
Yeah, something like that. Hey, you want that pickle?

He grabs the pickle spear before Yuri can answer.

Roe and Frank discuss their plans. Frank has his notebook out, pointing to a certain page containing an extensive list of bank names and street addresses.

                          FRANK
That's the complete list.

                          ROE
What are these names off to the side here?

                          FRANK
Names of all the employees and their schedules.

                          ROE
And you just walk in and take it?

                          FRANK
Two million. All there.

                          ROE
Unbelievable. I never thought I'd see the day. I think I was becoming
institutionalized in there.

                          FRANK
Did anyone bring my maps in?

                          ROE
No, I don't think so.

                          FRANK
Tony.

                          TONY
Yeah?

                          FRANK
Go back out to the truck and pull my case with all the maps.

                          TONY
Let me finish my fries.

                          FRANK
It won't take you but a minute. They're not going anywhere.

Tony places his fries down in disgust and walks to the door.

                          ROE
Dell, plug in the radio.

                         DELL
Don't have it.

                          ROE
Where is it?

                         DELL
The truck. Backseat floorboard. I told Tony to get it.

                         TONY
You did not!

                         DELL
I guess you couldn't hear 'cuz you was too busy griping.

                         TONY
I had good reason. You—

                          ROE
You're wasting time, Tony. Just get the maps and the radio.

                         TONY
Alright, alright.

Tony exits. The storm is worsening.

                          ROE
Smart-mouthed kid.

                         FRANK
Take it easy on him. He's part of the reason why we have two million
waiting for us. We're going to need him. You think Dell looks
trustworthy?

                          ROE
Has he always given everyone this much attitude?

                         FRANK
Not always.

                          ROE
He better be careful. It's not wise to upset Dell.

                         FRANK
Dell wasn't my call.

                    ROE
What did you want me to do? He was going to blow the whole thing
if I didn't cut him in.

                    FRANK
Empty threats.

                    ROE
Says you. But I didn't want to take the chance.

                    FRANK
Luck favors the prepared. Always have a contingency plan, for the
unexpected.

                    ROE
Yeah, him being here was definitely unexpected. I never have trusted
him.

                    FRANK
I never trust anyone.

                    ROE
Except Tony.

                    FRANK
That's different.

                    DELL
Hey Roe, when are we getting outta here?

                    ROE
In a couple of hours. I want to hear if there's any news on the breakout.
We need to know if any checkpoints have been set up.

                    DELL
You wouldn't even have to worry about checkpoints had we kept
driving. But now we're sittin' here with our dicks in our hands doin'
nothin'.

                    ROE
You want something to do? You and Yuri start getting that body outta
here.

Yuri jumps up and walks to the back room. Dell rises from the table, swallows
his last bit of food and lets out a loud belch.

YURI

That's nice.

DELL

Ahhh, even better the second time.

Tony re-enters with the RADIO and another small BRIEFCASE, identical in look to the one Frank stored in the bedroom.

FRANK

How is it out there?

TONY

Getting worse.

ROE

Let me have the radio.

Tony hands the radio over to Roe, and gives the briefcase to Frank. Roe plugs in the radio and tunes the dial. The crackle and hiss of static comes through the speaker.

Dell and Yuri make their way through the room with the body.

YURI

It's going to be hard to get anything in this area.

More hiss, then MUSIC. Everyone stops to listen. The music fades, replaced by a DEEJAY'S voice.

DEEJAY (V.O.)

That was Mozart's Piano Concerto Number 23 in A Major.

DELL

How are you gettin' a signal way out here?

FRANK

Must be from a station in Billings.

DEEJAY (V.O.)

It's now five o'clock and time for our evening newsbreak. Top story: Authorities are still searching for five convicts who escaped from a state penitentiary four days ago. The escapees were last seen on Highway 220 heading north, but authorities now believe that the group is involved with the disappearance of a Casper man, whose name police have yet to release. In other news—

> TONY
>
> Dammit Dell! They already know about the murder!

> ROE
>
> (to Dell and Yuri) You guys finish up.

Dell and Yuri haul the corpse to the front door.

Tony paces nervously.

Frank looks out the window.

> TONY
>
> (to himself) They know where we are. They're going to find us, then they're going to add murder on to my sentence.

Frank crosses to Tony.

> FRANK
>
> You have to calm down. Trust me.

> TONY
>
> This money was supposed to be ours. You never asked me what I thought before involving these other guys.

> FRANK
>
> I know. We're going to take care of it. Stick to the plan.

> TONY
>
> You never value anything I have to say.

> FRANK
>
> Just give it a few more days and we'll all be on a plane to Europe, or South America, or wherever.

> TONY
>
> Frank, don't talk to me like I'm twelve. I'm in this for the money, not murder. This got a whole lot more complicated when Dell took that guy out.

The front door is open. Yuri pulls on his half of the corpse. Dell stops.

DELL

Someone's coming.

TONY

What?

ROE

Get back inside! Shut the door!

Yuri and Dell shuffle back into the cabin. Roe closes the door. Frank peers out the window. An OLD MAN approaches. Tony paces nervously in the middle of the room.

FRANK

It's the caretaker.

ROE

How do you know?

FRANK

I saw him in the office on the way in.

ROE

Tony! Clean up these wrappers.

Tony grabs the discarded hamburger wrappers, stuffing them into his pockets. Dell and Yuri place the corpse into the back room.

ROE

Frank and I stay out here. The rest of you guys get in the back room.

Dell and Yuri recede into the shadows of the back room. Tony switches the radio off before joining them. Frank and Roe wait. There's a loud KNOCK at the door. Roe answers it.

OLD MAN

Evening.

ROE

Come in. Don't want you to freeze out there.

OLD MAN

Thank you.

The Old Man enters. Roe closes the door.

OLD MAN

Weather's gettin' pretty bad. Just you and your friend here?

ROE

Yes sir.

The Old Man looks around.

OLD MAN

Whoo! Smells like death in here.

Awkward pause.

FRANK

What can we do for you?

OLD MAN

My name's Hugh Cantrell. I'm the caretaker here. Chevy said some newcomers had arrived today.

FRANK

I believe he was the one we met when we picked up the key. Tall? Thick, gray beard?

OLD MAN (HUGH)

That's Chevy. Wanted to come up and meet you boys and welcome you to the campground.

ROE

We appreciate it.

HUGH

Also wanted to make sure you had everything you needed.

Hugh walks toward the back. Dell, Yuri and Tony wait in suspense.

FRANK

We're fine.

HUGH

Looks kinda sparse.

ROE

We'll be all right.

HUGH

Just concerned, is all. The general store is short on supplies. Haven't been able to get restocked since the storm came in. Took us all by surprise.

FRANK

I'm sure.

HUGH

How long you fellas planning to stay with us?

FRANK

Only a day.

HUGH

That so?

FRANK

We want to make sure we arrive in Gering by Thursday. Have to stay on schedule.

HUGH

Gering? I get up that way every few years, when I have the chance. Good fishing up there.

ROE

Don't let us keep you, Mr. Cantrell. I'm sure you have other obligations. We'll be fine.

HUGH

All right. But let me know if I can do anything for you. My cabin is the next one down from the store—on the right.

FRANK

Sure.

Roe walks Hugh to the door. Tony accidentally bumps a small table. Dell's KNIFE falls to the floor. Hugh turns.

ROE

Frank, see what that was.

Frank walks around the corner, out of sight.

ROE
What was it Frank?

FRANK (O.S.)
One of my flashlights rolled off the table. No damage done.

Frank returns. Hugh looks to the floor and notices a pale HAND jutting out. He swallows hard.

HUGH
Uh, well, I hope to see you boys around.

Hugh disappears into the snow storm. Dell, Yuri, and Tony emerge from the back.

DELL
(shoving Tony) What was that?

TONY
(shoving back) Hey, lay off! You think I meant to do it?!

DELL
Big mistake!

Dell lunges at Tony. A fight erupts.

FRANK
Stop it! Step back, both of you!

Dell slashes at Tony with his knife, misses, and hits Frank in the upper arm.

Frank staggers back.

DELL
This kid is a jinx. I told you he'd screw everything up.

TONY
What?!

FRANK
Would someone just get a towel.

Dell exits to find a towel. Yuri steps in with one.

                              YURI

Never mind Dell.

                              ROE

How does it look?

                              FRANK

It's not too bad.

                              ROE

I'll take care of it, Yuri. You and Dell have to get that body out of
here. Now.

                              YURI

Yeah.

INT. BACK ROOM.

Yuri crosses to the corpse. He sees the hand, lying in plain view of the front
door. Dell chews on Tony's french fries, listening to classical music on the
radio.

                              DELL

How do people listen to this?

                              YURI

(to Dell) Did you move the body?

                              DELL

What do you mean?

                              YURI

The body. Have you moved it since that Old Man was here?

                              DELL

Hey, I ain't done nothin'.

                              YURI

Then we might have a problem.

                              DELL

What do you mean?

Yuri points. Dell looks at the hand, then the front door.

                            DELL
If he saw anything, I swear he won't be tellin' anybody about it.

                            YURI
That's right, killing is the solution to all of life's little problems.

                            DELL
It keeps people from talkin'.

                            YURI
It also leaves a trail. Think about where we are. People like this old
guy are gonna be missed real quick.

                            DELL
It don't matter to me.

                            YURI
It matters to me, because I want see that money, and if you want your
cut, it better start mattering to you, too.

INT. LIVING ROOM.

Roe examines Frank's wound.

                            ROE
This cut is pretty deep. I think you're going to need stitches.

                            FRANK
There's a first-aid kit in the kitchen. Cabinet in the corner. Top
shelf.

Roe rises and crosses to the kitchen. Tony steps in to examine Frank.

                            ROE
(to himself) How the hell did he know that?

INT. BACK ROOM.

Yuri and Dell discuss the situation. Roe walks up.

                            ROE
I thought you two were going to get rid of that body.

                            YURI
Yeah, about that.

INT. LIVING ROOM.

Tony looks around to make sure none of the others are listening.

>   TONY
> I can't stay here much longer.

>   FRANK
> You'll be fine.

>   TONY
> How can you stay so calm?

Frank shrugs.

>   FRANK
> Experience.

>   TONY
> I'll never forget Lake Tahoe. Out on Lamoreaux's house boat. I didn't think he'd make the deal.

>   FRANK
> But he did. The plan was faultless.

>   TONY
> As always. Did you give Roe the story?

>   FRANK
> Of course.

>   TONY
> And the amount?

>   FRANK
> Two million.

>   TONY
> Only two? That's a stretch, isn't it?

>   FRANK
> It's believable. They'll be satisifed with their take.

>   TONY
> Leaves more for us.

                          FRANK
     I've always looked out for our interests. Your shoe is untied.
Tony looks down at his heavy, very distinct HIKING BOOTS. He leans over
to tie the left shoelace.

                            ROE
     Frank!

Frank rises and walks to the

BACK ROOM.

No one notices the corpse's hand twitch.

                           DELL
     How's the arm?

                          FRANK
     I'll live. Where's the first-aid kit?

                            ROE
     I got sidetracked. Yuri thinks the Old Man saw the body.

Tony rushes in.

                          TONY
     He saw the body?

                            ROE
     Maybe.

                          TONY
     Oh, that's beautiful.

Tony walks over to the windows and peers out.

                          FRANK
     We don't know for sure, so it's pointless to worry about it. Let's take
     one thing at a time. Just get the body out of here.

Dell and Yuri bend down to get the corpse. It jerks. They drop it to the floor.
The tarp unravels, exposing the man's contorted face.

                          YURI
     He's not dead!

                              TONY
Oh my god, he's still alive!

                              DELL
Shut up, I'll take care of it!

                              FRANK
Everyone calm down!

                              TONY
Do something!

                              YURI
He scared the hell out of me!

                              ROE
Get him out of here!

During the chaos, a GUNSHOT. Dell has shot the man right in the face.
BLOOD splatters on Tony's jacket.

Long pause.

                              ROE
Dump the body and clean this up. We're leaving—now.

The Deejay cuts through with an update.

                          DEEJAY (V.O.)
We have just received word from the State Board of Transportation
that all roads north of Worland are closed due to a severe winter storm.
Again, all roads, including interstates and county highways, have been
shut down due to inclement weather. Everyone in the listening area
is advised to wait until the storm subsides. We will bring you more
updates as they are issued from the National Weather Service.

                              DELL
(to Frank) Was this little layover on the schedule?

EXT. CABIN—NIGHT

A few hours have passed. Visibility is low. Yuri and Dell have finished burying
the body.

                              DELL

He ain't going anywhere now.

                              YURI
I'll put the shovels back into the car.

                   INT. LIVING ROOM.

Frank, arm now bandaged with GAUZE, lays his briefcase onto the table and opens it. Inside, neatly packaged, are various MAPS and CHARTS. He selects one and opens it.

                              TONY
What do we do now?

                              ROE
We can still make it out in that S.U.V.

                              FRANK
The route has to be carefully planned.

                              TONY
Let's just go now.

                              FRANK
We can't. It would be useless to get a mile down the highway and run into a roadblock.

                              TONY
We haven't heard anything about any roadblocks on the radio.

                              FRANK
I'm not necessarily talking about police roadblocks. I'm talking about iron gates that are used every winter to seal off impassible highways.

                            [MORE]

CHILDREN'S FICTION WINNERS

1 Alice Anne Ellis
Richmond VA

2 Gregory Fields
Ft Lauderdale FL

3 Lindsay Eland
Breckenridge CO

4 Selene Castrovilla
Island Park NY

5 Gerald Winter
Lakehurst NJ

6 D'Arcy A. Pryciak
Redford MI

7 Jessica Broyles
Titsuville FL

8 Sue Doucette, Leigh J. Friedman
Glenmore PA

9 Lynne Sella
Susanville CA

10 Stephanie Golightly Lowden
Madison WI

11 Victoria E. Miller
Glendale AZ

12 Josephine Nobisso
Westhampton Beach NY

13 Winnie Anderson
Baltimore MD

14 Nancy Werley
Sturgeon Bay WI

15 Amy Chiasson
Waltham MA

16 Rosanne Lindsay
Fitchburg WI

17 Daniel A. Miller
La Habra CA

18 Syrl Ann Kazlo
Foet Ann NY

19 Lynn Montgomery
Santa Barbara CA

20 Kate Dunn
New York NY

21 Tracy L. Smith
Mechanicsville VA

22 Kimberly Silver
Newburgh IN

23 Rhonda Leverett
The Woodlands TX

24 Laurie Alloway
San Diego CA

25 Kanika Wright
Bronx NY

26 Kathleen T. Pelley
Greenwood Village CO

27 Gregory Stephen Fields
Ft Lauderdale FL

28 Rebecca Rowley
Greeley CO

29 Patricia Casson Henderson
St Johns NF Canada

30 Carolyn Whitaker
St Louis MO

31 Kimberley Alcock
Delta BC Canada

32 Beth Hope-Cushey
Monongahela PA

33 Cheryl Bardoe
Chicago IL

34 Candie Moonshower
Nashville TN

35 Tamara Molyneaux
Jasper TX

36 Jean Reagan
Salt Lake City UT

37 Judith Millar
Kitchener ON Canada

38 Barbra Hesson
Calgary AB Canada

39 Lisa Prince-Smith
Chugiak AK

40 Robert Sweeten
Seneca MO

41 Lisa Colangelo
Chicago IL

42 Cathy Stefanec Ogren
Waunakee WI

43 Scott Openshaw
Draper UT

44 Joyce Pyka
Stickney IL

45 I. Wes Murrell
Baltimore MD

46 George Youngblood
Spring TX

47 Margaret M. Mahoney
Scranton PA

48 Rita White
West Hollywood CA

49 Cheryle T. Williams
Jupiter FL

50 Karen Beaumont
San Martin CA

51 Amy Moore
Natick MA

52 Paula Wynne
Berkshire United Kingdom

53 Paula Wynne
Berkshire United Kingdom

54 Lisa Finnegan
Columbus OH

55 Leanna M. McGee
Springfield IL

56 Tina M. Vannatter
Tomahawk WI

57 Barb Lutarewych
Ft Myers FL

58 Mark Friedlander
McLean VA

59 Randi Lynn Mrvos
Lexington KY

60 Samuel L. Williams
Williamstown NJ

61 Amy F. Whitt, Eugene Apow
Rocky Mountain House AB Canada

62 Patricia G. Schofill
Margate FL

63 Angela Haliburda
Lansing MI

64 Genelle Morain
Athens GA

65 Ken Kilback
Burnaby BC Canada

66 June E. Clark
Ft Worth TX

67 Gus Maples
Lucedale MS

68 Lindsay Eland
Breckenridge CO

69 Kim DeLeo
Wyoming MN

70 Kathleen Palm
Woodburn IN

71 Karen Beaumont
San Martin CA

72 Nancy Churnin
Plano TX

73 Pamela Bloom
Forest Hills NY

74 Deborah Ader
Rockville MD

75 John M. Prophet
Harwich MA

76 Katy Donahue-Cavazos
Albuquerque NM

77 H. Carolyn Jones-King
Columbia MO

78 Josephine Pasquarelli
Kennedy Township PA

79 Margaret M. Mahoney
Scranton PA

80 Ronald L. Roehrich
Portland OR

81 Ronald L. Roehrich
Portland OR

82 Stephen J. Tomasi
Bakersfield CA

83 Cama Duke
Boone NC

84 Laurie Hopkins
Clearwater FL

85 Barbara Long
Pioneer TN

86 N.M. Shukla
San Jose CA

87 Laird Roberts
Salt Lake City UT

88 Verona Morse
Northville MI

89 Stephanie Johnson
Salt Lake City UT

90 Jack Vaughan
Springfield VT

91 Nora Rock
Ajax ON Canada

92 Pamela Hill
Leesburg FL

93 Mayra Calvani
St Stevens Woluwe Belgium

94 Susan Rosson Spain
Conyers GA

95 Peggy House
Perrinton MI

96 Angela K. Small
West Hartford CT

97 Frank P. Humphreys
Chiswick London UK

98 Iliana Pappas
New York NY

99 Amy Chiasson
Waltham MA

100 Verna Safran
Sarasota FL

FEATURE ARTICLE WINNERS

1 Christy Heitger-Casbon
Noblesville IN

2 Martha W. Murphy
Narragansett RI

3 Heather K.W. Brown
Acworth GA

4 Matthew Tuthill
Bennington VT

5 William M. Holden
Fair Oaks CA

6 John Henry Sotomayor

7 Geri Hoekzema
Vancouver WA

8 Cora Schenberg
Charlottesville VA

9 Fiona Shen
Eden Prairie MN

10 Laura Shumaker
Lafayette CA

11 Liz Fleming
St Catharines ON Canada

12 Kathleen D. Anderson
Akron OH

13 John Henry Sotomayor

14 Tom Lavagnino
West Hollywood CA

15 Ron Gompertz
Camas WA

16 Ron Gompertz
Camas WA

17 Martha W. Murphy
Narragansett RI

18 Linda Hagen Miller
Spokane WA

19 John Henry Sotomayor

20 Mike Jernigan
Kaneohe HI

21 Patricia Casson Henderson
St Johns NF Canada

22 Linda Hagen Miller
Spokane WA

23 David Copeland
Burlington MA

24 Pamela R. Corante
Hermosa Beach CA

25 Joanne Cronrath Bamberger
Chevy Chase MD

26 Karen Hammond
S Bristol ME

27 Maria Pascucci
Lancaster NY

28 Andes Hruby
Canaan CT

29 Larry McMullen
Bensalem PA

30 F.T. Laskin
Angels Camp CA

31 John McCaa
Irving TX

32 Russell W. Estlack
St George UT

33 Alvin Hattal
Kirkland WA

34 Dorothy Pedersen
Orangeville ON Canada

35 Douglas W. Bower
Guanajuato, GTO

36 Matthew Stabley
Washington DC

37 Marie Mischel
Midvale UT

38 Ellen Sagmyr
Emigrant MT

39 Cheryl Caruolo
Whitman MA

40 Alvin Hattal
Kirkland WA

41 JoAnne Tobias
San Francisco CA

42 Linda Moor Anelli
West Dover VT

43 LaVada Davis
Elizabeth IN

44 Meredith Vasquez
Panguitch UT

45 Kelly Cunningham
Cambridge MA

46 Lisa Capone
Melrose MA

47 Christine Mattice
Hartville OH

48 Hilary Hansen
Reisterstown MD

49 Janet Mendelsohn
West Somerville MA

50 Donna M. Recktenwalt
Dayton OH

51 Sandra Chambers
Wilmington NC

52 Maria Pascucci
Lancaster NY

53 Anita Boser
Issaquah WA

54 Andes Hruby
Canaan CT

55 Katherine Yurchak
Muncy PA

56 Kim O'Connell
Arlington VA

57 Rick Ramseyer
Cumberland Center ME

58 Janis L. McLaughlin
Wellington OH

59 Jennifer Lacey
Minneola FL

60 Donna M. Recktenwalt
Dayton OH

61 Jessica McCann
Scottsdale AZ

62 Layla Revis
Los Angeles CA

63 Harriet Epstein
Floral Park NY

64 Joanne Cronrath Bamberger
Chevy Chase MD

65 Ginger Dehlinger
Bend OR

66 Theresa Cianciolo
San Diego CA

67 William J. Walker
Crowley TX

68 Monica Morris
Los Angeles CA

69 Karen Peters
Coeburn VA

70 Brunetta Two Lenz
Las Vegas NV

71 Roberta Gastineau
Kotzebue AK

72 Jessica McCann
Scottsdale AZ

73 Kaye Patchett
Tucson AZ

74 Noble Collins
Payson AZ

75 Mike Kielkopf
Waterloo IA

76 Connie Albrizio
Windsor CT

77 Clifford A. Porter
Everett WA

78 T.C. McClenning
Canton GA

79 Maria DeLong
Tulsa OK

80 Ramsey Harris
Athens GA

81 Elizabeth Orendorff
Uniontown AR

82 Kathryn Witt
Covington KY

83 Jim Woodard
Ventura CA

84 Dave Wiley
Chesterland OH

85 Carole Carson
Nevada City CA

86 Barbara Anton
Sarasota FL

87 Barbara Anton
Sarasota FL

88 Fiona Worboys
Chicago IL

89 Kimn Swenson Gollnick
Marion IA

90 David John Rippe
Cheyenne WY

91 Sandra Chambers
Wilmington NC

92 Sondra H. Kahn
La Jolla CA

93 Danette Haworth
Orlando FL

94 Cynthia Lane
Bradenton Beach FL

95 Danette Haworth
Orlando FL

96 Linda Dees
Madison AL

97 Alex Gabbard
Lenoir City TN

98 Bonnie Fewins
Miles City MT

99 Peggy Jaeger
Keene NH

100 Susan Duke
Peoria IL

GENRE SHORT STORY WINNERS

1. **Rachael M. Haring**
   Cliffwood NJ
2. **David Sakmyster**
   Penfield NY
3. **James Philip Cox**
   Pasadena CA
4. **R. Michael Burns**
   Gainesville FL
5. **Tommie Spear**
   Pasadena CA
6. **Daryl Sedore**
   Barrie ON Canada
7. **Mark Daugherty**
   Staunton VA
8. **Justin Pilon**
   Tainan City Taiwan
9. **Richard Murphy**
   San Augustine TX
10. **Lauren Kellogg**
    Jamison PA
11. **Anne-Marie Yerks**
    Ferndale MI
12. **David Carr**
    El Cerrito CA
13. **Jim Baker**
    Perth Australia
14. **Susan Budavari**
    Fountain Hills AZ
15. **Gillian Niven**
    Sydney NSW Australia
16. **Daryl Sedore**
    Barrie ON Canada
17. **Karen Sandler**
    Cameron Park CA
18. **Anna Foster**
    Wahiawa HI
19. **Don Michael Kearby**
    Caddo TX
20. **Frances E. McGee-Cromartie**
    Dayton OH
21. **Mark Torrender**
    Watford Herts UK
22. **Scott Crowder**
    Douglasville GA
23. **K.B. Keilbach**
    Irvine CA
24. **Robert W. Liddell**
    Valley Stream NY
25. **Henry Hack**
    Miller Place NY
26. **Salvatore Amico M. Buttaci**
    Lodi NJ
27. **Bo Braze**
    Meridianville AL
28. **Henry Hack**
    Miller Place NY
29. **Karma L. Wright**
    Alvin TX
30. **Peter G. Thomas**
    Streator IL
31. **Daryl Sedore**
    Barrie ON Canada
32. **Stephanie Burkhart**
    Castaic CA
33. **Nathan Woodson**
    Monroe NC
34. **Jeremy Girard**
    Sounderstown RI

35. **Robin Valaitis Heflin**
    Camano Island VA
36. **Mark Daniels**
    Corbin KY
37. **Christopher J. Caramsalidis**
    MA
38. **Tim Franklin**
    Canton MI
39. **Lydia DeBlock**
    Saskatoon SK
40. **Jeremy Moyes**
    Brandon FL
41. **Gordon Kelley**
    Evansville IN
42. **Mark Quinn**
    Naperville IL
43. **Samantha Gregory**
    Diamondhead MS
44. **Dee Hogan**
    Leavenworth KS
45. **Nancy Quatrano**
    Hastings FL
46. **Tracy Jones**
    Martinsville IN
47. **Judi Roberts**
    Springville IN
48. **William Frankl**
    Wynnewood PA
49. **Kate Harris Richardson**
    Havre MT
50. **Jeremy Girard**
    Sounderstown RI
51. **Robert Mayer**
    Santa Fe NM
52. **Salena Marie Barrett**
    Stockbridge GA
53. **Daryl Sedore**
    Barrie ON Canada
54. **Sheila Prevost**
    Wellsboro PA
55. **Margot Richter**
    Granite Falls MN
56. **Shirley Radlove**
    Covington KY
57. **Debra R. Shipman**
    Lancaster SC
58. **Warren Doman**
    Concord Twp
59. **Caroleah Johnson**
    Berry Creek CA
60. **Daryl Sedore**
    Barrie ON Canada
61. **Donna MacNaughton**
    Brooks AB Canada
62. **Paige Roberts**
    Round Rock TX
63. **Debbie Pierce**
    Mattoon IL
64. **Ray Verola**
    Oakdale PA
65. **Veronica Arteseros**
    Delran NJ
66. **Sandra D. Dorsett**
    Montgomery TX
67. **Steven Sparks**
    Columbus OH
68. **Vickey Malone Kennedy**
    Norman OK

69. **Catriona Ling**
    Mosman Australia
70. **Shannon Sorrels**
    Ashburn VA
71. **Avis Dillon**
    Albany NY
72. **David Carr**
    El Cerrito CA
73. **Sue A. Lehman**
    Lower Lake CA
74. **Melissa Maher**
    Dallas TX
75. **Melissa Gould**
    Windham NH
76. **James R. Gilliam**
    Colorado Springs CO
77. **Gene Alvin**
    Collinwood TN
78. **Robert Trist**
    Gindig Queensland Canada
79. **Elizabeth Miravalle**
    Clearlake Oaks CA
80. **Jim Boan**
    Bloomfield MO
81. **Edmund X. DeJesus**
    Norwood MA
82. **Terry W. Sako**
    Wheatfield IN
83. **Jyothi Kuruvilla**
    Bolingbrook IL
84. **Joan Cathcart**
    Ventura CA
85. **Martine Ehrenclou**
    Los Angeles CA
86. **Robert Jellicoe**
    Kingston ON Canada
87. **Phyllis Washburn**
    Marion MA
88. **Robert Huck**
    Skokie IL
89. **Janetta Messmer**
    The Woodlands TX
90. **Elaine Marlier**
    Littleton CA
91. **Beverly Cazzell**
    Dayton OH
92. **Edmund X. DeJesus**
    Norwood MA
93. **Charles Brown**
    Millersville MD
94. **Judith Fawley**
    Pensacola FL
95. **Alicia Stankay**
    Ambridge PA
96. **Jose Villegas**
    Mathis TX
97. **Lance Erlick**
    Rolling Meadows IL
98. **Anne-Marie Yerks**
    Ferndale MI
99. **Vonda D. Garrett**
    Troy AL
100. **Shirley Radlove**
    Covington KY

INSPIRATIONAL WRITING WINNERS

1   Jan Ledford
    Franklin NC

2   Fay Wentworth
    Meyersdale PA

3   Margie Kiefer
    North Mankato MN

4   Rhonda Larson
    Soldotna AK

5   Anita Tarlton
    Wadesboro NC

6   R. Wayne Stockdale
    Cornelius NC

7   Karen Witemeyer
    Abilene TX

8   Susan M. Watkins
    Woodstock GA

9   Carla Cook
    Hope ID

10 Reg Ivory
    Johnson City TN

11 Lori M. Henry
    Bear DE

12 Robbie Jeanne Baylor
    Thomasville NC

13 Rev. Lyn G. Brakeman
    Gloucester MA

14 Elizabeth MacDonald Burrows
    Seattle WA

15 Karen Laskowsky
    Woodbridge VA

16 L.A. Coutu
    Richmond VA

17 Arlene Smith
    Nepean ON Canada

18 Leslie W. Pickering
    Atlanta GA

19 Janet Feldman
    Las Vegas NV

20 Peggy Jaeger
    Keene NH

21 Rev. Lyn G. Brakeman
    Gloucester MA

22 Donna M. Trickett
    Grove City OH

23 Cherilyn DeAguero
    San Clemente CA

24 Miriam Hill
    Clearwater FL

25 Margie Chellete-Clifton
    Dodson LA

26 Nancy Costa
    Thousand Oaks CA

27 Peggy Eastman
    Chevy Chase MD

28 Frances Turney
    Grants Pass OR

29 Fran Palumbo
    San Francisco CA

30 Joan C. Metzger
    Flower Mound TX

31 Michael Taylor
    Henderson NV

32 Gale Limbacher
    Lakeville MN

33 Nathan Dempsey
    Oak Hill OH

34 Tiffany Stuart
    Colorado Springs CO

35 Nelson Chamberlain
    Brighton CO

36 Laurie Klein
    Deer Park WA

37 Judy Woodward Bates
    Dora AL

38 Cyndi Struven
    Goleta CA

39 Marisa Daugherty
    Mount Vernon TX

40 Terry Nelson
    Omaha NE

41 Brenda Stinnett
    Tracy CA

42 Pam Vaughan
    Stow MA

43 Sherry Elaine Eubank
    Estill Springs TN

44 Terry Harris
    Huntington Beach CA

45 Elvira Nado
    Suffern NY

46 Eleanor W. Cunningham
    Gathersburg MD

47 Lisa Begin-Kruysman
    Bay Head NJ

48 Randy Brown
    Ames IA

49 Linda Voncile Roberts
    Barnhart MO

50 Cristine A. Gruber
    Riverside CA

51 Alissa Dunn
    Woodstock GA

52 Jim Puckett
    Bentonville AR

53 Jennifer Oakes
    Lexington KY

54 Irene Metellus
    Parker CO

55 Nancy Corley
    Rutherford TN

56 Art Lester
    Torremolinos Spain

57 Anastasia Foster
    Benton TN

58 George Jones
    Leeds AL

59 Alice R. Marks
    Colorado Springs CO

60 Scott Wilke
    Campbellsport WI

61 Connie Barber
    Eatontown NJ

62 Danny Wright
    China Spring TX

63 Candace Sorondo
    Ridgefield Pk NJ

64 Laurel Karry
    Carlisle ON Canada

65 Donna David McCubbibins
    Irmo SC

66 Ronald Stout
    Canal Winchester OH

67 Steven M. Ward
    Gainesville GA

68 J.K. Jackson
    Springfield OR

69 Julie Alexander
    Pasadena CA

70 Tamitha Curiel
    Garland TX

71 Dennis J. Sylvia
    Phoenix AZ

72 James Crosby
    Lumberport WV

73 Tom Kelly
    Appleton WI

74 Keri L. Johnson
    Renton WA

75 Desiree Middleton
    Plantation FL

76 Jon F. Voss
    Prairie Village KS

77 John Paul Godges
    Santa Monica CA

78 Ruth Ann Cornelson
    Mukilteo WA

79 Shirrell Z. Bond
    Lubbock TX

80 Terry A. Shear
    Swanton OH

81 Mary Moss
    Richmond VA

82 Bonnie Atkins
    Holyoke MA

83 Alece B. Egan
    Navasota TX

84 Robert Hunt
    Schererville IN

85 Sandra Wood
    Mission Viejo CA

86 Laurie Perkins
    Needham MA

87 Vic Bodine
    Trenton NJ

88 Jennifer Floyd
    Papillion NE

89 Wendy M. Lee
    Miramar FL

90 Anne Warren Smith
    Corvallis OR

91 Wayne Faust
    Evergreen CO

92 Shirley Rawlins
    Riverton UT

93 Cindy
    Armada MI

94 Cynthia Lane
    Bradenton Beach FL

95 Ann Champeau
    Norman OK

96 April Laverriere
    Biddeford ME

97 Neena Kahlon
    Fort Worth TX

98 Barbara Tuttle
    Lansing MI

99 Monica Moore
    Tappahannock VA

100 Christine Anderson
    Morristown NJ

MAINSTREAM/LITERARY SHORT STORY WINNERS

1 **Carol Manley**
Springfield IL

2 **Renee Thompson**
Folsom CA

3 **Carol Manley**
Springfield IL

4 **Patricia Bownas**
Poughkeepsie NY

5 **J. Alan Smothers**
Glendale AZ

6 **Anthony Lagler**
Scio OR

7 **Bernice Brooks Bergen**
Sarasota FL

8 **Gala White**
Corunna MI

9 **Joseph C. Prindle**
Santa Monica CA

10 **Laura Lagana**
Duluth GA

11 **Jerry Foshee**
Rio Rancho NM

12 **Barbara Anton**
Sarasota FL

13 **Renata Pipkin**
Roxana IL

14 **Gabrielle Fox**
Mt Kisco NY

15 **Richard Gibney**
Co Dublin Ireland

16 **Barbara F. Seiden**
Southfield MI

17 **Barbara Anton**
Sarasota FL

18 **Jay R. Hodes**
Sherman Oaks

19 **Genetta Adair**
Eads TN

20 **Amy Cissell**
Los Angeles CA

21 **Robert Sweeten**
Seneca MO

22 **Dolly Dennis**
Edmonton AB Canada

23 **Marianna DiGiammo**
Hull MA

24 **Suzanne Schryver**
Merrimack NH

25 **Douglas S. Meyers**
Cincinnati OH

26 **Nolcha Mir Fox**
Playa Del Rey CA

27 **Nikki Andrews**
Wilton NH

28 **Alla Crone**
Santa Rosa CA

29 **Carol Manley**
Springfield IL

30 **Tim J. Rocheford Jr.**
Zimmerman MN

31 **Michelle Featherston**
Pawnee IL

32 **Kathryn Ardell Meyer**
Argyle NY

33 **Shelley Muniz**
Columbia CA

34 **Cynthia Pryor**
Powell OH

35 **Barbara Anton**
Sarasota FL

36 **Deborah Klein**
Edmond OK

37 **Vinny Sea Ciambriello**
Brooklyn NY

38 **Monica Morris**
Los Angeles CA

39 **Richard Gibney**
Co Dublin Ireland

40 **Mal King**
Santa Paula CA

41 **Jonathan Roberts**
Plainfield IN

42 **Carol Manley**
Springfield IL

43 **Richard Gibney**
Co Dublin Ireland

44 **J. Brook Seaford**
Matthews NC

45 **Rick Rogich**
Arlington Heights IL

46 **Tracy Franklin**
Toronto ON Canada

47 **Gueh Yanting**
Singapore

48 **Nina Schloesser**
Brooklyn NY

49 **Deanna Richards**
Brooklyn NY

50 **Andrew W. Campbell**
Raleigh NC

51 **Carol Manley**
Springfield IL

52 **Monica Morris**
Magnolia IL

53 **Randy Susan Meyers**
Boston MA

54 **Tim Hicks**
Denman Island BC Canada

55 **Randy Susan Meyers**
Boston MA

56 **Stephen J. Tomasi**
Bakersfield CA

57 **Jamie Tyo**
Seattle WA

58 **L.B. Gschwandtner**
Stafford VA

59 **Daniela Petrova**
New York NY

60 **Warren H. Albrecht**
Fargo ND

61 **Monica Morris**
Magnolia IL

62 **Judy S. Dodd**
Spartanburg SC

63 **Phil Slott**
Kamuela HI

64 **Danny Wright**
China Spring TX

65 **Susan Surman**
Winston-Salem NC

66 **Judy Goldman**
Wyoming PA

67 **J.A. Buxton**
Sebastopol CA

68 **Randy Susan Meyers**
Boston MA

69 **Aoise Stratford**
Ithaca NY

70 **Keri Austin**
Red Deer AB Canada

71 **Jill Renee Walsh**
Meridian MS

72 **Fred L. Edwards, Jr.**
South Pasadena FL

73 **Peter Philipps**
Bethesda MD

74 **Ann L. Camy**
Morrison CO

75 **Betsy Graziani Fasbinder**
Nevada City CA

76 **Judy S. Dodd**
Spartanburg SC

77 **Andrea Hill**
Gaithersburg MD

78 **Robin Beaman**
Studio City CA

79 **Susan Duke**
Peoria IL

80 **Rena Moore**
Grantham PA

81 **Peter Philipps**
Bethesda MD

82 **Robert Sweeten**
Seneca MO

83 **Myron Stokes**
Dayton OH

84 **Bernice Brooks Bergen**
Sarasota FL

85 **Clare Blando**
Kansas City MO

86 **Jim Thomson**
South Portland ME

87 **Dale Myers**
Ventura CA

88 **John L. Williams**
Tucson AZ

89 **Lance Erlick**
Rolling Meadows IL

90 **Claire Hsu Accomando**
Bonita CA

91 **Paige Jones**
Sanford FL

92 **Phillip Henry**
Medford MA

93 **Julie Felhofer**
Marshfield WI

94 **Robert Sweeten**
Seneca MO

95 **Leann Austin**
Randolph NY

96 **Eliko Kosaka**
Tokyo Japan

97 **Anelise Smith**
Claremont CA

98 **Juliet Krassenstein**
Bradfordwoods PA

99 **Mary Brewster**
Santee CA

100 **Aprille Janes**
Port Perry ON Canada

MEMOIR/PERSONAL ESSAY WINNERS

1 Jasmin Darznik
   Tiburon CA
2 John Becknell
   La Jolla CA
3 Larry Connolly
   San Francisco CA
4 Laghretta Daniels Bell
   Gainsville FL
5 Kimberli R. Pedley
   Auburndale FL
6 Harry Browne, MD
   Sparks NV
7 Barbara W. Richard
   Sequim WA
8 Lillian Schaie Mattimore
   The Sea Ranch CA
9 Lucille Bellucci
   Oakland CA
10 Mary Emerick
   Sitka AK
11 Donna DiMenna
   St Paul MN
12 Carrie Friedman
   Los Angeles CA
13 Geri Hoekzema
   Vancouver WA
14 Tracy Gary
   New York NY
15 Juliet M. Hanna
   Denver CO
16 Robert G. Johnson
   San Antonio TX
17 Audrey Bastian
   Provo UT
18 Jackie Lantry
   Rehoboth MA
19 Ross McPhail
   Salt Lake City UT
20 Barbara Bamberger Scott
   Dobson NC
21 D.S. Bell
   Stockbridge GA
22 Lauren Morales
   Merrick NY
23 Robert Chute
   London ON Canada
24 Barbara Lewis
   San Francisco CA
25 Diana Keyes
   Middletown CT
26 John R. Cusack
   Isle of Palms SC
27 Aurelia C. Scott
   Portland ME
28 Ellen Sagmyr
   Emigrant MT
29 Vicki Carter
   Galveston TX
30 Paulle Clark
   El Prado NM
31 Anne M. Luna
   Alhambra CA
32 Fatima Rashid
   Ocala FL
33 Kara Jane Rollins
   Alameda CA
34 Joyce Garner
   North Truro MA

35 Minnie Davis
   Lexington MA
36 John J. Di Sanza
   Dunedin FL
37 Bebe Fish
   Miami FL
38 Linsley Fleur Bock
   Sedro Woolley WA
39 Maryann De Leo
   New York NY
40 Terry Cox-Joseph
   Newport News VA
41 Laura Shumaker
   Lafayette CA
42 Veronica Breen Hogle
   Buffalo NY
43 Toni Francis
   Dickinson ND
44 Art Lester
   Torremolinos Spain
45 Georgette Beck
   Marblehead MA
46 Debby Farrow
   E Haddam CT
47 Julie Matlin
   Montreal QU Cnada
48 Lizzie Hannon
   Santa Rosa CA
49 Edward H. Garcia
   Dallas TX
50 Shaun Patrick Attwood
   Tucson AZ
51 Marilyn Hanna
   Freeport NY
52 James Gish, Jr.
   Arcanum OH
53 Kathryn Presley
   Bryan TX
54 Robert Hart
   Daytona Beach FL
55 Elsie Schmied Knoke
   Oak Ridge TN
56 Colleen Plimpton
   Bethel CT
57 Janice Airhart
   Broken Arrow OK
58 Donna DiMenna
   Saint Paul MN
59 Elizabeth King
   Los Angeles CA
60 Audrey Martin
   Berkeley CA
61 Meredith Guest
   Petaluma CA
62 Jo Hedges
   Marquard South Africa
63 Ashley Johnson
   Downers Grove IL
64 Ralph Spinelli
   Vallejo CA
65 Ann Marie Falcone
   Cleveland Heights OH
66 Sarah Kaufman
   Altavilla CA
67 Juan J. Hinojosa
   Austin TX
68 Teresa Hubley
   Oakland ME

69 Joseph P. Ritz
   Hamburg NY
70 Seantee Campbell
   Miramer FL
71 Bertha Zuniga Campos
   Harlingen TX
72 Kay Cumnock
   Mesquite TX
73 Anne DeLaet
   Tyler TX
74 Marji Butler
   Chester CT
75 George Altman
   Clermont FL
76 Julie Lynch
   Minnetonka MN
77 Brian Mullally
   Cobourg ON Canada
78 Andes Hruby
   Canaan CT
79 DeAnn Knight
   N Little Rock AR
80 Erec Toso
   Tucson AZ
81 Susan Scharfman
   Boynton Beach FL
82 Michael Higgins
   New York NY
83 Katie McCollow
   Minneapolis MN
84 Willma Willis Simpson Gore
   Sedona AZ
85 Barbara Anton
   Sarasota FL
86 George Griggs
   Citrus Heights CA
87 Cheryl Romo
   San Pedro CA
88 Carolyn Stewart
   Pensacola FL
89 Bob LaBelle
   Schererville IN
90 Milt Lowe
   New York NY
91 Alex Gabbard
   Lenoir City TN
92 Richard Palombi
   Belton TX
93 Kathleen T. Pelley
   Greenwood Village CO
94 Tova Gabrielle
   Berkeley CA
95 Craig C. Garner
   West Chester PA
96 Daniel F. Rousseau
   West Palm Beach FL
97 Robin Holleran
   Mendham NJ
98 Eva D. Haddix
   Creamery PA
99 Charles Novacek
   Detroit MI
100 Doris Butt
   Milan IN

NON-RHYMING POETRY WINNERS

1	Judith Hemenway Del Mar CA	35	Donald Hewlett Ann Arbor MI	69	Patricia Dreyfus Corona Del Mar CA
2	Susan Warfield Minneapolis MN	36	Yvonne Nunn Hermleigh TX	70	Joan Marg Levittown NY
3	Carolyn Kreiter-Foronda Hardyville VA	37	Brenda Frezell Lansing MI	71	Ethel M. King Haymarket VA
4	Maria Ercilla Los Angeles CA	38	Chris Lord Ann Arbor MI	72	Emily Jiang Mountain View CA
5	Annabelle Moseley Dix Hills NY	39	Lizzie Hannon Santa Rosa CA	73	Judith Stock Boonville MO
6	Gloria Masterson Richardson Rockport MA	40	Jennifer Lynn Holley Old Saybrook CT	74	Pamela S. Loy Los Angeles CA
7	Diane C. Marty Dowagiac MI	41	Jerry Nash Cookeville TN	75	Sherry Hardage Los Alamos NM
8	Sheila A. Murphy Portland CT	42	Cong Xiao River Edge NJ	76	Joan Huffman Wallingford PA
9	Rashna Owens Castro Valley CA	43	Dorien K. Miles Bremerton WA	77	Kenton Wing Robinson West Hartford CT
10	Patricia R. Bush Scottsdale AZ	44	Dory Alvaton KY	78	Muhammad Bashir St. Petersburg FL
11	Lisa Marie Webster Burbank CA	45	Joni Kingland Boise ID	79	Nan Salomon Spartanburg SC
12	Kathleen M. Curry Blue Mountain Lake NY	46	Martin A. Ramos Hormigueros PR	80	Carol Manley Springfield IL
13	Jane Morgan Shippensburg PA	47	Lylanne Musselman Indianapolis IN	81	Carol Manley Springfield IL
14	Andrew B. Pierce Miami FL	48	Rebecca Vaupotic Portland OR	82	Carol Manley Springfield IL
15	Thomas M. McGlaughlin, Jr. Philadelphia PA	49	Stephanie Pearson Kuna ID	83	Deloris Gauntlett Kingston 8 Jamaica
16	Sheila Forsyth Irvington NJ	50	Mollie Crisp Pasadena MD	84	Jacqueline Neron Hughesville PA
17	Alison Luterman Oakland CA	51	Jason Tutone La Mesa CA	85	Margaret A. Morris Leesburgh FL
18	Tina Ganguly Brooklyn NY	52	Shakuntala Rajagopal Algonquin IL	86	Carol Mann La Quinta CA
19	Karen D. Mitchell Indianapolis IN	53	Gloria Masterson Richardson Rockport MA	87	Manuel Figuroa Del Norte CO
20	Lesley Kellas Payne Fresno CA	54	Chandi J. Wyant Louisville CO	88	Ann-Marie Legan Herrin IL
21	Maggie Lawrence Tucson AZ	55	Maggie Lawrence Tucson AZ	89	Carolyn Luke Brantford ON Canada
22	Maria Ercilla Los Angeles CA	56	Janet Stevenson Chelmsford MA	90	Joyce Keveren Phoenix AZ
23	Bruce Rolfe Livingston TX	57	Maria Ercilla Los Angeles CA	91	John Oliver Mason Philadelphia PA
24	Marilyn E. Churchill Ann Arbor MI	58	Lylanne Musselman Indianapolis IN	92	Clif Mason Omaha NE
25	Sister Dorothy Forman, OSF/T Tiffin OH	59	Lesley Kellas Payne Fresno CA	93	Mary T. Ruffin Ashland VA
26	Ida Isabel Donohue Alhambra CA	60	Joan Higuchi West Islip NY	94	Mary T. Ruffin Ashland VA
27	Susan Warfield Minneapolis MN	61	Rose Lobel Santa Cruz CA	95	Laura Purdie Salas Maple Grove MN
28	Fabio Cardoso Honolulu HI	62	Jeanne M. Park San Diego CA	96	Laura Purdie Salas Maple Grove MN
29	Kelsey Bernier Brooklyn CT	63	Lois Mintah Washington IL	97	Carol Manley Springfield IL
30	Ann R. Langdon New Haven CT	64	Rita McCord Cedar Rapids IA	98	Chandi J. Wyant Louisville CO
31	Virginia Fortner Shawnee Mission KS	65	Ruth Kibler Peck Dayton OH	99	Maggie Lawrence Tucson AZ
32	Dorothy Brummel Sunrise FL	66	Geri Hoekzema Vancouver WA	100	David Prinz Hufford Omaha NE
33	Juanita Kirton E Stroudsburg PA	67	Liz Mowrey Weiser ID		
34	Bonnie McMeans Havertown PA	68	Ana Maria Nezol Salem OR		

RHYMING POETRY WINNERS

1   Rebecca Foust
Ross CA

2   Melissa Cannon
Nashville TN

3   N. Colwell Snell
Salt Lake City UT

4   JoAnne Growney
Silver Spring MD

5   Melissa Cannon
Nashville TN

6   R. Asher Ausbrooks
Gerlach NV

7   R. Asher Ausbrooks
Gerlach NV

8   Patricia Callan
Newton MA

9   William A. Abbott
Tacoma WA

10   Nancy Jean Carrigan
Warrenville IL

11   Robert Daseler
Davis CA

12   Carla Conley
Morganton NC

13   Teena Roemer
Pagosa Springs CO

14   Carole J. Fincher
Memphis TN

15   Joan Higuchi
West Islip NY

16   Jean Stem
Akron OH

17   Patricia Callan
Newton MA

18   Robert Russell Marquardt
Skagway AK

19   Janis Marler
Brick NJ

20   Altha Murphy
Imboden AR

21   Verda S. Boyd
Penney Farms FL

22   Patricia Callan
Newton MA

23   Patricia Callan
Newton MA

24   Annabelle Moseley
Dix Hills NY

25   Annabelle Moseley
Dix Hills NY

26   Annabelle Moseley
Dix Hills NY

27   Suellen Wedmore
Rockport MA

28   Beth Wells
Louisville KY

29   Gene Dixon
Pitman NJ

30   Caitlin Doyle
East Hampton NY

31   Caitlin Doyle
East Hampton NY

32   J.H. Grimson
Kenosha WI

33   Tara Grover
Paradise CA

34   Patricia Callan
Newton MA

35   Robert Russell Marquardt
Skagway AK

36   Graal Braun
St Petersburg FL

37   Patricia Callan
Newton MA

38   Patricia Callan
Newton MA

39   Robert Daseler
Davis CA

40   Bethany
Atkinson IL

41   Vonda D. Garrett
Troy AL

42   Lorna R. Ellis
Houston TX

43   Maril Crabtree
Mission KS

44   Ann-Marie Legan
Herrin IL

45   N. Colwell Snell
Salt Lake City UT

46   N. Colwell Snell
Salt Lake City UT

47   N. Colwell Snell
Salt Lake City UT

48   Suellen Wedmore
Rockport MA

49   Rebecca Foust
Ross CA

50   Annabelle Moseley
Dix Hills NY

51   Pamela Dane Hayes
Battle Creek MI

52   Pamela Dane Hayes
Battle Creek MI

53   Kristen R. Wilson
Getzville NY

54   Cynthia Scott
Provo UT

55   Melissa Cannon
Nashville TN

56   Melissa Cannon
Nashville TN

57   Annyce Eaton-Carson
S Stone Mountain GA

58   Annyce Eaton-Carson
S Stone Mountain GA

59   Toni Blake
Granbury TX

60   Toni Blake
Granbury TX

61   Richard Bilby
Lawton OK

62   Michael L. Neff
Wilton WI

63   Paul Christian
Macon GA

64   Robert Russell Marquardt
Skagway AK

65   Dianne Borsenik
Elyria OH

66   Cynthia Scott
Provo UT

67   Margaret Bzan
Canton OH

68   Connie Wiedeman
Kailua HI

69   Jeffrey Kuczmarski
Chicago IL

70   Rebecca Foust
Ross CA

71   Emily Jiang
Mountain View CA

72   Valma M. Bartlett
Oak Harbor WA

73   Valma M. Bartlett
Oak Harbor WA

74   Cordell Caudron
Lewiston ID

75   Jim Hiner
Belmont WI

76   Patricia Fain Hutson
Newport VA

77   Gail White
Breaux Bridge LA

78   Phil Cerasoli
San Diego CA

79   Ann-Marie Legan
Herrin IL

80   Maureen Cannon
Ridgewood NJ

81   Edna Cabcabin Moran
Alameda CA

82   Ernestia Fraser
Nassau Bahamas

83   Shirley Underwood
Van Nuys CA

84   Marian Wilson
Tucson AZ

85   Larry Groves
Madison AL

86   William Sowell
Deland FL

87   Patricia R. Bush
Scottsdale AZ

88   Janelle Smith
Miami FL

89   Anna Amatuzio
New York NY

90   Rhonda Leverett
The Woodlands TX

91   Bob Hackney
Daly City CA

92   John Mace
Union City NJ

93   Kevin Sulzberger
Overland Park KS

94   Alex Gabbard
Lenoir City TN

95   Yusef Mitchell
NY

96   Jeanne M. Park
San Diego CA

97   George N. Braman
Bronx NY

98   Sharon Harris Warrick
Jacksonville FL

99   Janelle Smith
Miami FL

100   David L. Meek
Knob Noster MO

STAGE PLAY SCRIPT WINNERS

1. Cary Pepper
   San Francisco CA
2. Anita Chandwaney
   Chicago IL
3. Michael P. Dooner
   Athlone Ireland
4. Mark Daniels
   Corbin KY
5. Nicolette Vajtay
   North Hollywood CA
6. Lori Taylor
   Chicago IL
7. Jake Broder
   London England
8. Rob Egginton
   Astoria NY
9. Marcia R. Rudin
   New York NY
10. Gary Miller
    Georgetown TX
11. Carrie Schule
    Memphis TN
12. Bernadette E. Smith
    Hathaway Pines CA
13. Keisha Poiro
    Great Mills MD
14. Jan O'Connor
    North Hollywood CA
15. Terry Anne Sachko
    Albuquerque NM
16. Mark Lambeck
    Stratford CT
17. Amy Dominy
    Phoenix AZ
18. Cathy Conger
    Wisconsin Rapids WI
19. Jim Gustafson
    Wheaton IL
20. Terrance Mahady
    Bush LA
21. Kristof Bathory
    New York NY
22. Alvin Schnupp
    San Luis Obispo CA
23. Mary W. Bruton
    Paris France
24. Susan Surman
    Winston-Salem NC
25. Marcia Corbino
    Sarasota FL
26. Dan Blackley
    Chino Hills CA
27. Alvin Schnupp
    San Luis Obispo CA
28. Ron Hill
    Old Fort OH
29. Mary Caudle-Silveira
    San Luis Obispo CA
30. Mary Clever
    Salinas CA
31. Jeremy Sony
    Columbus OH
32. Linda S. Barnes
    Wilmington NC
33. Ann Reckling
    Barned KS
34. Grace M. Topping
    Fairfax Station VA

35. Antonio Donata, NBCT
    University Place WA
36. Nick Vigorito, Jr.
    Brooklyn NY
37. Paula Newberry
    Memphis TN
38. Ken Pisani
    Van Nuys CA
39. Mary Lee Costa
    Brooklyn NY
40. Tiffany Antone
    Los Angeles CA
41. Glorida Cosgrove
    Port St Lucie FL
42. Katherine Pellettiere
    Chicago IL
43. R.C. Hooker
    Somers MT
44. Stephen Cvengros
    Redmond WA
45. George Kirazian
    San Diego CA
46. Chris Kent
    Irvine CA
47. Chris DiGiovanni
    Toluca Lake CA
48. Debra Doggett
    Durango CO
49. Colleen Summa
    Rego Park NY
50. Jerome Brown
    Grove City OH
51. Linda Mitchell
    New Albany MS
52. Deborah Gray
    Lafayette IN
53. Jack Marshall
    Bangor ME
54. Debra Doggett
    Durango CO
55. Peter Budka
    Washington DC
56. George Rothman
    Irvine CA
57. Robert Lynn
    Dubuque IA
58. Malvin Wald
    Sherman Oaks CA
59. Todd McGinnis
    Brampton ON Canada
60. Clifford W. Smith
    Gainesville GA
61. Mary Beth Hoerner
    Chicago IL
62. Ken Levens
    Redding CA
63. Jonathan David Sloate
    Greenwich CT
64. Edmund L. DuBois
    Sonoma CA
65. George Taylor
    Beaverton OR
66. Phillip Schmiedl
    New York NY
67. Barbara Tylla
    Racine WI
68. Kathleen Tomko
    Brookings OR

69. Dylan Guy
    New York NY
70. Don Orwald
    Granbury TX
71. Pat Hart
    Cleveland OH
72. Don Orwald
    Granbury TX
73. Dale R. Botten
    Quinn A. Williams
    Superior WI
74. Dennis E. Rager
    Bronx NY
75. Keisha Poiro
    Great Mills MD
76. John T. Costello
    Fresno CA
77. Donna Drake
    Locust Grove GA
78. Jonathan Janssen
    Lancaster CA
79. Corinne Brown
    Allen Park MI
80. Jann Correll
    Oxnard CA
81. Valerie Stulman
    Riverside CA
82. Richard C. Johnston
    Columbus OH
83. Alexa Alexander
    Arcadia CA
84. Tevia E. Abrams
    New York NY
85. Lynn Veach Sadler
    Sanford NC
86. Fred de Luna
    West Linn OR
87. Jonathan David Sloate
    Greenwich CT
88. Barbara Summers
    Forest Grove OR
89. Mark Lambeck
    Stratford CT
90. Mike Gilfillan
    Navarre FL
91. Robert Emmett Lunney
    New York NY
92. Don Orwald
    Granbury TX
93. Vanda
    New York NY
94. Kathleen Tomko
    Brookings OR
95. Jeanne Dube-Herrero
    Fernandina Beach FL
96. Brian Wizard
    Wallawa OR
97. Brian Wizard
    Wallawa OR
98. Andrew M. Barbolla
    San Diego CA
99. Julie Macmanus
    Halifax NS
100. Dianalee Velie
     Newbury NH

TELEVISION/MOVIE SCRIPT WINNERS

1 **Clint Till**
Birmingham AL

2 **Cynthia Webb**
Helena MT

3 **Jacqueline Frazier**
Venice CA

4 **Neil Gaughan**
Los Angeles CA

5 **Daniel Ellis**
Ringgold GA

6 **Marc V. Calderwood**
Albuquerque NM

7 **Vanessa Rojas**
Valley Village CA

8 **Brad Barth**
Roslyn Heights NY

9 **Jen Klein**
Lake Balboa CA

10 **Anthony R. Benitez**
San Marcos TX

11 **Neil Gaughan**
Los Angeles CA

12 **Brad Barth**
Roslyn Heights NY

13 **Carlo Decarlo**
Rutherford NJ

14 **Sid Smoliga**
West Linn OR

15 **Michael L. Brown**
Chatsworth CA

16 **Jen Stansfield**
Parker CO

17 **William B. Huelsenkamp**
Louaine C. Elke
Bandon OR

18 **Evette Vargas**
Toluca Lake CA

19 **Lamar Jeffcoat**
Columbia SC

20 **M. Ivan Kander**
Waterford VA

21 **Kelly Allen**
Los Angeles CA

22 **Anthony R. Benitez**
San Marcos TX

23 **Shirley Ware**
Seville OH

24 **Blas E. Padrino**
Orlando FL

25 **Anne Porter Paris**
Mayville NY

26 **Uri Miron**
New York NY

27 **Brian Keith Smith**
Lone Tree IA

28 **John R. Leyva**
Colton CA

29 **John Lewis**
Metamora MI

30 **Carol M. Adorjan**
John M. Adorjan
Glenview IL

31 **Alisan Peters**
Jackson WY

32 **Sejal B. Ravani**
Los Altos CA

33 **Troy Tradup**
Saint Paul MN

34 **Peter Phelan**
New York NY

35 **Dion Owens**
Chicago IL

36 **Anne Krumrey**
Valley Village CA

37 **Keisha Poiro**
Great Mills MD

38 **Nick Korolev**
Martinsburg WV

39 **John K. Herr**
Alexandria VA

40 **Bethany Patchin Torode**
S Wayne WI

41 **Ron Nason**
N Vancouver BC Canada

42 **Candace Rose**
Phoenix AZ

43 **Keri Austin**
Red Deer AB Canada

44 **Dian D. Perrin**
Baltimore MD

45 **Anita J. Skibski**
Algonquin IL

46 **David Huffman**
Colorado Springs CO

47 **Sid Smoliga**
West Linn OR

48 **Harry Bauer**
Chicago IL

49 **Joel Betancourt**
West Palm Beach FL

50 **Ron Basso**
Richard Brooks
Virginia Beach VA

51 **Susan Keogh**
Flint MI

52 **Julie Anne Wight**
Burbank CA

53 **John Merenda**
Iverness FL

54 **Ann Metcalf**
Vineyard Haven MA

55 **Edward Johnson Jr.**
Butner NC

56 **George Baxter**
Cresskill NJ

57 **Julie Anne Wight**
Burbank CA

58 **Meredith Guest**
Petaluma CA

59 **Carol A. Hanrahan**
Scottsdale AZ

60 **Debra Deaver**
Viroqua WI

61 **Corinne McAfee**
St Louis MO

62 **Meredith Averill**
Los Angeles CA

63 **Jay S. Blumenkopf**
Boca Raton FL

64 **Valerie Stulman**
Riverside CA

65 **Rafael Aguilo**
Los Angeles CA

66 **Kahron Spearman**
APO AE

67 **Katherine Wolff**
Altamonte Springs FL

68 **Susan Beth Lehman**
Wayne PA

69 **Jullian Kingsford**
Ogden UT

70 **Marilyn Moriarty**
Roanoke VA

71 **Jullian Kingsford**
Ogden UT

72 **Christopher Grimesey**
Middleburg Hts OH

73 **Sammy Montana**
Long Beach CA

74 **Pamela Nelson**
Littleton CO

75 **Laurence Brenner**
New York NY

76 **Suzanne Tedesko**
Seattle WA

77 **Gerard Brown**
Kennesaw GA

78 **Michael North**
Los Angeles CA

79 **Dugan McKenzie**
Albion ME

80 **Roland T. Quesada**
Weslaco TX

81 **Joyce E. Britton**
Texas City TX

82 **Tom Patterson**
Atlantic Highlands NJ

83 **Michael Rascona**
Holtsville NY

84 **Christy Lynn Anana**
Snohomish WA

85 **Tom Smith**
Anthem AZ

86 **Denis J. Harrington**
Fx Station VA

87 **George Baxter**
Cresskill NJ

88 **Katherine T. Koonce**
Coral Springs FL

89 **Renee Rankin**
Oakland CA

90 **Jeremy Hoffpauir**
Lubbock TX

91 **Thomas Mollica**
West Milwaukee WI

92 **Phyllis Allison**
Los Angeles CA

93 **Thomas Mollica**
West Milwaukee WI

94 **Robert Allen Finan**
Lakewood OH

95 **Kristin Roybal**
San Jose CA

96 **Jennifer Johans**
Phoenix AZ

97 **Patrick Kendrick**
West Palm Beach FL

98 **Christopher W. Williams**
West Newton MA

99 **Sharon Contillo**
Coventry RI

100 **Brian Grose**
Warrensville Hts OH

DISCOVER HOW EASY
PUBLISHING YOUR BOOK
CAN BE

Available at Amazon.com
for $5.95 or as a free
e-book at
www.OutskirtsPress.com